Knowledge

Management

U N L O C K I N G

>K_n_o_w_l_e_d_g_e>>

A S S E T S

Solutions

from

Microsoft

Susan Conway
Char Sligar

PUBLISHED BY
Microsoft Press
A Division of Microsoft Corporation
One Microsoft Way
Redmond, Washington 98052-6399

Library of Congress Cataloging-in-Publication Data
Conway, Susan, 1947-
    Unlocking Knowledge Assets / Susan Conway, Char Sligar.
      p. cm.
    Includes index.
    ISBN 0-7356-1463-6
    1. Knowledge management.   2. Organizational effectiveness.   I. Sligar, Char.   II. Title.

  HD30.2 .C655   2002
  658.4'038--dc21   2001057961

Printed and bound in the United States of America.

1 2 3 4 5 6 7 8 9   QWT   7 6 5 4 3 2

Distributed in Canada by Penguin Books Canada Limited.

A CIP catalogue record for this book is available from the British Library.

Microsoft Press books are available through booksellers and distributors worldwide. For further information about international editions, contact your local Microsoft Corporation office or contact Microsoft Press International directly at fax (425) 936-7329. Visit our Web site at www.microsoft.com/mspress. Send comments to *mspinput@microsoft.com*.

Acquisitions Editor: Alex Blanton
Project Editor: Jenny Moss Benson

Body Part No. X08-29518

To my husband, Jack, whose loving support makes
all things possible, and our greatest assets,
our children, Mara and Adam.
—Susan Conway

To my children, Dayna and Kyle, who are my assets,
and to Al, who represents the highest form
of human capital.
—Char Sligar

Contents

Part II
The Process of Knowledge Management

Part III
The Technology of Knowledge Management

Foreword

For the leading practitioners of knowledge management (KM) at Microsoft to write a book is, if you'll forgive the expression, a no-brainer. Here is one of the fastest-growing and most successful knowledge-based enterprises in the world. Here is one of the most prolific producers of software—a knowledge product if ever there was one—on the planet. Here is a company renowned for the raw intelligence and accumulated knowledge of the fortunate individuals who become its employees. Here is a company used as a poster child for the value of intangible assets—a company where, even in a down economy, market value exceeds book value many times over. Microsoft is a knowledge-oriented company in a knowledge-oriented industry in a knowledge-oriented economy, and we should all be interested in how this company manages its knowledge.

That said, even if you have zero interest in Microsoft as a company, you'll still find *Unlocking Knowledge Assets* useful. Its recommendations would also work in, say, a tractor manufacturing company. There is little or no marketing hype for Microsoft products or services—just an occasional subtle mention of them where appropriate.

Beyond the fact that it's written by experts at Microsoft, what is special about this book? It's important to note first that Microsoft's conventional wisdom about KM is by and large consistent with the world's conventional wisdom. It's generally agreed throughout the known universe, for example, that the human side of knowledge is more difficult to "manage" than the technical side, and I was reassured to find out that even these Microsofties concur in this assessment. There are extensive chapters on culture and communities, and even in the more technical sections of the book one never forgets that it is people who make KM successful (or unsuccessful). In general the approach is mainstream, and adopting the tenets from the book will not get you fired. Just the opposite, in fact. If you internalize the messages and approaches herein, you'll possess more solid know-how than 99 percent of the knowledge managers in the Western world.

Another piece of good news is that this is a "second generation" approach to KM. Microsoft wasn't the first company to adopt KM or to build its capabilities into software products. But now, almost a decade after the earliest efforts to manage knowledge, Microsoft is clearly one of the leading users of KM (it's a perennial high-scorer in the "Most Admired Knowledge Enterprises" awards, for example), and many of its products now incorporate high levels of KM functionality. Following the proven approaches presented in this book ensures that you won't pursue a once-promising approach that didn't quite pan out.

Some of the book would be familiar to anyone who's reviewed the rest of the KM literature. Still, this content is useful for all but the most sophisticated knowledge managers, and even they can be assured that no important aspect of the subject has been skipped. Readers will discover that even the familiar subjects come with more useful implementation detail than they've ever seen elsewhere. You may feel that you know about "communities of practice" (Chapter 5, "Creating and Sustaining Communities of Practice"), for example, but it's unlikely that you've ever seen the key roles in communities broken down by typical responsibilities and the time commitment they require. It's always clear what "step 1," "step 2," and so on are.

But there are several chapters of the book that cover material available, to my knowledge, nowhere else. The book takes a strong value orientation throughout, but Chapter 2, "Placing a Value on Your Knowledge Management Investment," presents a unique, state-of-the-art model (developed in conjunction with Baruch Lev, the leading thinker on intangible assets) for measuring the value of knowledge to the organization. The model is driven by the specific behaviors that would change if knowledge were deployed successfully within an organization. While it's still early days for the model, I have considerable hopes for its broad application in companies other than Microsoft.

The book's focus on technology, which comprises three chapters and various comments throughout the other sections, also distinguishes it from the rest of the KM literature. Most KM authors either skip the technology issue altogether or provide only a few vague generalities on the topic. *Unlocking Knowledge Assets* covers the subject in considerable depth, from the overall KM architecture to detailed repository and search tool alternatives. Despite the fact that many people minimize the importance of technology to KM, it's the most tangible way to approach a knowledge initiative. If you're going to do KM, you're going to do knowledge technology—and this is a rare source of expertise on the topic.

One of my favorite chapters is Chapter 6, "Building Taxonomies." I know of no other source on the subject, which is extremely important as content proliferates and the ability to find a particular knowledge object becomes more challenging. I have spent a little time with the Knowledge Network Group at Microsoft, which manages the largest intranet site at the firm. It's the most sophisticated group of KM taxonomy-builders I've ever come across. They make the "librarianship" of knowledge assets into a high art. Fortunately, their approaches are described for the first time in print in this book. Like the rest of the content, there is all the detail any reader could desire. I was unaware, for example, that there were ANSI and ISO standards for "Guidelines for the Establishment and Development of Monolingual (and Multilingual, for that matter) Thesauri," but they are mentioned briefly in this chapter. I wasn't even sure that "thesauri" was the plural of thesaurus!

There are other, smaller gems. The "knowledge index"—a high-level outline of potential knowledge that guides knowledge asset development—is described in Chapter 7, "Capturing Your Organization's Knowledge Assets," and creating one strikes me as a very good idea. Another helpful tool is the common framework, called the "Knowledge Cycle," used throughout the book to place specific topics in context and orient the reader. Because almost every chapter utilizes the framework, it gives the book a cohesion not often found with multiple authors.

In short, I think that *Unlocking Knowledge Assets* is a great addition to the KM literature and a source from which anyone interested in the subject would benefit. Just to prove my objectivity, I will say that I would like to have read even more about the specific KM situation at Microsoft. I would also have liked to learn about how Microsoft determines and keeps track of what knowledge its people have and how it has been so successful at hiring people with the knowledge it needs. But a more Microsoft-centric book might have deterred some readers, and now something is left for the next book!

THOMAS H. DAVENPORT

Acknowledgments

Writing this book would not have been possible without the knowledge exchange and dedication of numerous individuals whose contributions made the task of representing the multiple paths to knowledge management (KM) within Microsoft clear and presentable. We thank them all for their invaluable assistance.

We especially want to thank the members of the Microsoft Consulting Services (MCS) Knowledge Management team for their unwavering support and valued contributions. Their nearly three-year journey on the KM road was the foundation and inspiration for this book. We would like to thank Steven Wright and Joel Shalaby for working through most of the technology materials in Part III, and Ursula Hildenbrand, Graham Watson, and Roberta Croly for their contributions to the content on communities of practice and content management in Part II. We are indebted to the MCS KM development team for developing and maintaining the project and providing technical information and moral support—Mark Davies, Ameya Bhalavdekar, Janine Crumb, Charles Ofori, and Dhilip Gopalukrishnan. A note of thanks to Bob Forgrave for contributing and aligning the quotes in each chapter to the content and to Kimberly Bell for her insights into the organization and change management issues.

Without the knowledge and support of the MCS field organization, this book would not have been written. Content, ideas, and specific contributions were received from around the world. So many of our consultants contributed to this book that making a complete list would be impossible, but we would like to specifically thank the following consultants who contributed content and significant time to the effort:

- MCS UK practice: Callum Shillan, Darren Strange, David Preedy
- MCS South Africa practice: Danny Venables
- MCS Columbia practice: Fernando Vallejo
- MCS U.S. Philadelphia practice: Dinesh Kumar
- MCS U.S. Connecticut practice: Kevin Morris
- MCS U.S. MidWest practice: Scott Andersen
- MCS DK practice: Anders Bjørn Skjønaa

These MCS consultants spent many hours of their personal time contributing to and refining our ideas, and perhaps most important, challenging our words. We sincerely appreciate their effort.

We want to acknowledge all the contributors in Microsoft's Product and Headquarters groups for providing product-specific information and ideas and for reviewing segments of the work as it was completed. Leading the list are Mary Lee Kennedy, Alex Wade, and Karen Eliasen from Human Resources Information Services group for their contributions in shaping the vision of corporate portals and taxonomy. Contributions and support from the Office team came from a number of people including Gail Thomas-Flynn, Gytis Barzdulas, and Jeff Teper from the Business Productivity group; Tom Moran, who provided insight into the public communities supported by Microsoft's Content Development & Delivery Group; Mark Mortimore, also from the CDDG group; and Shafeen Charania and Ahmad Abdel-Wahed from the CMO IT Infrastructure group for assisting in the development of the value model in Chapter 2. Jim Boyle, from the Windows Engineering Services group, provided product insight. Marc Smith and his team from Microsoft Research were kind enough to supply the information and support for the Netscan project that we gratefully included in our work. As with the people in MCS, these individuals believe in the importance of KM and have given generously of their time to support this project. We thank each of them for their support. We are grateful not only to the named contributors but to many others within our company who reviewed our manuscript and provided feedback during its evolution.

We greatly appreciate the support and knowledge exchange with Tom Davenport, Director, Accenture, Institute for Strategic Change. He was a valued part of the development effort. Professors Baruch Lev of the New York University Stern School of Management and Feng Gu of Boston University are greatly appreciated and valued for their review and feedback on our Intellectual Capital model.

Thanks also to Alex Blanton, who encouraged and administered this project, and Jenny Moss Benson, who patiently edited our work. We thank them for their patience with our unachievable deadlines and for all of their good work.

Finally, we thank our family and friends who supported us and gave us the time to complete this project. Without their tolerance and understanding this book would not exist.

Susan Conway

Char Sligar

Introduction

*The metaphysics of global power has changed. Markets are
now more valuable than territory, information more powerful than military hardware.*

Time Magazine[1]

The central message of this book is that knowledge—not money or technology—is the primary economic unit of business in the twenty-first century, and
that management of that knowledge is essential for any company that hopes
to compete effectively. In the late eighteenth century, the Industrial Revolution taught business managers that relying on mechanical engines and other
technology meant that those engines had to be primed, maintained, and managed to stay running and generate profits. In the early twenty-first century,
business managers are learning the same lesson about knowledge. The fuel for
the knowledge engine exists within every company, but that knowledge must
be accessed, organized, and managed for its spark to be ignited and its energy
to be used.

In 1997, *Fortune* magazine editor Thomas Stewart observed that "money
talks, but it does not think; machines perform, often better than any human
being can, but [machines and technology] do not invent....[The] primary purpose of human capital is innovation—whether of new products and services,
or of improvement in business processes."[2] This book argues that knowledge
management, or KM, is an engine that can drive this innovation by providing
a structured and visible means of unlocking a company's knowledge assets
(KAs). Access to and use of these assets will empower workers to create ever
more innovative products and services that build on their companies'
strengths.

Collaboration technology (such as Internet portals, workflow systems,
and massive multiformat storage devices) has shifted the economic emphasis
from tangible to intangible assets, resulting in pressure to change the way we
manage. Managing knowledge, in this new economy, will provide companies
with new opportunities to improve productivity and gain substantial competitive advantage. Throughout this book we seek to lead you through the options

---

1. Lance Morrow. Man of the Decade Gorbachev: The Unlikely Patron of Change. *Time*
   (Jan. 1, 1990).

2. Thomas Stewart. *Intellectual Capital: The New Wealth of Organizations.* London: Nicholas
   Brealey Publishing. 1998.

and implications of embracing knowledge management as a core company value and management philosophy. We will also look at the economic role of human capital (people) in a knowledge-based company. In light of this new view of the economic value model, we discuss the associated business culture, processes, and enabling technologies that represent the next step in organizational evolution—a step that will change not only the way people work but the way we all view work relationships.

We started this project a year ago to describe the processes, goals, and requirements of KM for Microsoft Consulting Services (MCS). Our clients and other groups within the company urged us to compile our findings in a format that could be shared by all. Why? In part, they saw the evolution of a framework for the implementation of value-based KM. They thought the framework was practical and could be used in their own organizations. Many of our clients are inundated by an endless parade of marketing materials lauding the next cure for the KM dilemma. Our promise to you is that we will offer more than just a list of technologies that you can use to solve a problem you are not even sure you have; we will give you an understanding of issues we see as a knowledge-based company and describe the ways we have sought to address these issues. We have attempted to describe the most common issues we have faced as one of the leading knowledge-based companies in the world, and allow you to benefit from our experience.

Our Assumptions About You

When we wrote the initial material that became the foundation for this book, we pictured our management team as our audience. Our team consisted of managers, developers, and consultants who made the decision to restructure the existing KM system. Throughout this book we have tried to relate our experiences with the issues that face organizations trying to embrace KM, as well as those seeking to move to a more collaborative KM model (from a basic portal or information-sharing stage). We have not dwelled on the technical issues that only experienced taxonomists or KM practitioners will be interested in. This book designed to give business decision makers an understanding of what this evolution means to both the organization and its employees.

As managers and sponsors of the shift to a knowledge-based organization, you should expect to benefit from this book in three ways: first, you should gain a clear understanding of the economic value of KM for your company. Second, you should be able to use the framework presented to develop a basic model within your own organization. Finally, you should be able to make a more effective investment decision as a result of understanding the forces, and not just the technology potential, that shape KM in an organization.

Organization of This Book

To accomplish our goals we have divided our work into three parts—strategy, process, and technology. The following figure shows each topic (with chapter number) and the corresponding conceptual relationships presented in the book under which the individual topics fall.

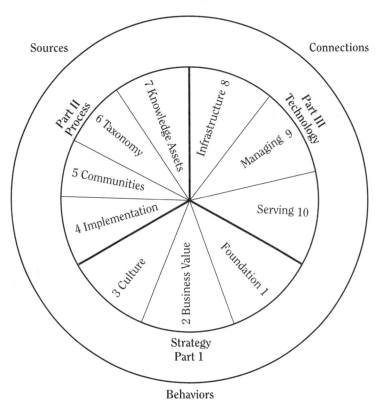

Figure 1.   *The Knowledge Management Elements Wheel*

Part I, "Knowledge Management as an Organizational Strategy," addresses KM as a strategy for your business and explores KM's role in the larger business environment. Chapter 1, "Knowledge Is the Foundation of Business," addresses what an organizational knowledge foundation is and what drives

KM for your organization. Chapter 2, "Placing a Value on Your Knowledge Management Investment," describes KM's economic imperatives and business value. And Chapter 3, "Knowledge and the Business Culture," explains the methods your organization should use to blend processes and systems to create an environment and a culture that support knowledge reuse.

Part II, "The Process of Knowledge Management," details the method of implementing a KM solution. Chapter 4, "An Implementation Framework," explains the elements of a solid process roadmap. Chapter 5, "Creating and Sustaining Communities of Practice," Chapter 6, "Building Taxonomies," and Chapter 7, "Capturing Your Organization's Knowledge Assets," describe how to build key elements of a KM solution: communities of practice, taxonomies, and knowledge assets.

Part III, "The Technology of Knowledge Management," covers the technology that a KM solution uses. Chapter 8, "Building a KM Foundation," Chapter 9, "Measuring the Effectiveness of Your Repository," and Chapter 10, "Knowledge Searching and Services," cover the technology needed to support the key elements of a knowledge engine: a repository to support content management, a search process to find knowledge assets, and an implementation management plan to fire up the engine.

Knowledge Management as an Organizational Strategy

*It was only with the coming of the Industrial
Revolution that the rate of change became
fast enough to be visible in a single lifetime.*

Isaac Asimov (1920-1992), American writer

Knowledge management (KM) is not a new term. Over the
past decade it has become a generic phrase used to refer to
many types of information exchange between people. In this
book, however, knowledge management has a specific meaning: the process of revealing and mapping the work activities,
behaviors, and knowledge sources within an organization.
The goal of a KM program is to relate the primary business
goals, or key performance indicators, of a company to:

- The *productivity* that results from employees performing work activities
- The *efficiency* gained through integrated processes
  the employees use to perform these activities or gain
  knowledge
- The *asset growth* (both tangible and intangible) that
  results from knowledge-based work activities

These goals can easily be seen in a simple product sales
scenario. A company account manager has a sales target to
generate each quarter for each account. The job of the
account manager is to call on customers and gain product
orders to meet his quota. The account manager uses his
knowledge of the product (gained through training, product
updates, and links to the product development staff), the
competition, and his customer to achieve his goal. The
required activities of calling on the customer and presenting an order form will most likely not result in a sale. If

product sales were this simple, e-commerce and telemarketing would have rendered the sales profession obsolete. In reality, the account manager must present himself at the opportune time (possibly having knowledge that the customer is experiencing an increase in market share for his or her own products or services), demonstrate knowledge of the competition's pricing and products (to point out the advantages of his own offering relative to the market), and offer timely access to inventory and discounting options from his or her own company. Armed with such knowledge, access to key information, and the ability to execute, the account manager is positioned to make the sale. This is the power of managing knowledge. In the knowledge era companies will either be competent consumers and producers of knowledge or they will be the victims of the competition's ability to harness this dynamically growing resource.

When thinking of harnessing any resource, your attention immediately turns to how it can be managed and with what tools you will accomplish the task. For most people KM brings to mind images of massive systems to gather and collate all the knowledge within a company. The truth is that KM systems range from simple Web sites (presenting information to employees) to fully integrated workflow environments (with software to allow workers to collaboratively manage documents or other asset production and use). Both of these approaches qualify as KM systems because they manage a company's knowledge—that is, the knowledge that is produced, consumed, and transformed into a company's products and services. As Figure I-1 shows, KM systems fall on various points along two planes: work behaviors and knowledge sources. The figure shows that the capacity to generate business value (in terms of the use of knowledge by employees) increases as knowledge moves from the personal, less structured spaces in the lower left corner to the public, more structured spaces in the upper right.

Knowledge is an individual asset, meaning that it is created at the individual level. The critical element in converting this asset into corporate value "depends on tapping the tacit and often highly subjective insights, intuitions, and hunches of individual employees and making those insights available for testing and use by the company as a whole…".[1] Consequently, organizations that rely heavily on collaboration seek to encourage the reuse and exchange of knowledge—a process that eventually extends the knowledge through the organization. Although all KM systems have collaborative elements, how much and how often people access the KM system depends on the company culture and how accountable workers are for seeking out and making use of knowledge that already exists.

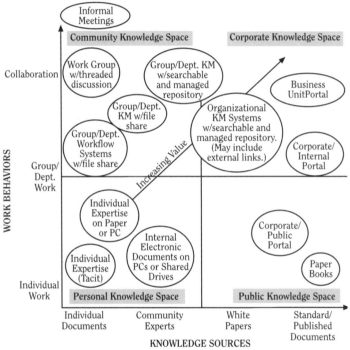

Figure I-1. *Knowledge Management Environment*

Figure I-1 shows that when the audience for knowledge is small, more focused KM solutions are used. These solutions can be as simple as a folder on a server that all people in a group can access, or a teaming application that appears on the users' desktop such as Microsoft SharePoint Team Services or Adobe Acrobat. Simple teaming applications generally are a low-cost solution; they have few options and work as add-on components

1. Ikujiro Nonoka. "A Dynamic Theory of Organizational Knowledge Creation." *Organization Science* 5, no. 1 (1994): 97.

to the common office desktop. These simple solutions work because the knowledge can be efficiently shared among a small group. In small groups it is easy to ask a peer for an explanation or find out if someone else is working on a document before you start to make changes to it. But these simple solutions are difficult to maintain across a large organization. The growth of collaborative technology, such as Microsoft SharePoint Portal Server, allows more collaboration in the larger corporate environment. This leap in technology is in turn enabling a increase in the amount of potential knowledge exchange in companies. As exciting as this concept sounds, managers will want to carefully align the company's goals with any proposed KM objectives to determine which type of knowledge they need to address first, and how much collaboration the company should strive to achieve.

Throughout this discussion of KM, it is important to remember that KM is not just a technology solution—that is, it is not about creating a database that simply collects and stores copies of documents that contain everything that employees know or that is embedded in the systems they use. On the contrary, KM is about embracing a diversity of knowledge sources and making the knowledge held in these sources available to employees in a timely and culturally acceptable manner. In short, the essence of KM is fueling what knowledge workers do best—what Microsoft's chairman and chief software architect Bill Gates refers to as "thinking work"—through blending a business's processes and corporate culture with the enabling technology to foster an innovative environment.

Organization of This Section

Throughout Part I we will address the fundamental drivers for managing knowledge in any organization. Chapter 1, "Knowledge Is the Foundation of Business," provides a foundation for understanding organizational knowledge. Chapter 2, "Placing a Value on Your Knowledge Management Investment" and Chapter 3, "Knowledge and the Business Culture," address the specifics of business value and the cultural drivers for KM within an organization.

Knowledge Is the Foundation of Business

Picture a building. Companies all added floors as they got bigger. Size adds floors. Complexity adds walls. We all built departments—transportation departments, research departments. That's complexity. That's walls. The job all of us have in business is to flatten the building and break down the walls. If we do that, we will be getting more people coming up with more ideas for the action items that a business needs to work with.

Jack Welch, Jr., CEO, General Electric[1]

You might be deciding whether to implement a **knowledge management (KM)** system in your business (or whether to convince others in your organization to do so). Before you make that case, it will help to understand the principles that underlie such a system. As we will see in this chapter, an effective KM system is more than just a fancy database used to store documents. To manage your organization's knowledge, you have to make it easy for employees to enter, store, and reuse all that information. This chapter shows how knowledge is valuable to an organization, how managing that knowledge becomes more important as the global economy evolves, how you can turn your organization's knowledge into value, and how a KM system can help.

The Value of Knowledge

Sharing knowledge of processes, roles, change, culture, products, and services with and by employees is the lifeline of any knowledge-based enterprise. That is because this basic company information represents not only the enterprise's business output but also the means to achieve it; in essence, corporate knowledge represents an enterprise's nonphysical (intangible) asset base—including the knowledge and experience of its people that can be captured in words, diagrams, code, equations, and so on.

---

1. *Fortune*, (December 30, 1991).

Knowledge by itself does not produce value, but when an organization collects the knowledge contained in its employees and processes, the organization can turn that knowledge into value. For example, when a company decides to upgrade one of its products, the product design team can review the list of implementation problems from the product's previous deployment to ensure that it does not repeat or compound the problems from the last version. The key to harnessing this value is making sure your organization's **knowledge sources**—documents, processes, designs, and so on—are mapped to collaborative, knowledge-based work behaviors, such as producing estimates for new work or designing new products. This process allows an organization to reuse its knowledge, which can increase productivity and free workers to devote their energies to innovation instead of reinvention.

Any organization can make its knowledge a renewable resource with unlimited growth potential as long as it encourages reuse of that knowledge. By reusing knowledge, workers can increase their productivity because they reduce the time it takes to gain information. The key to reusing knowledge is finding a way to filter and manage it. This is where a good **knowledge management system** can help.

Figure 1-1 shows a typical life cycle of reused knowledge. In this basic model the knowledge worker possesses knowledge based on his or her experience, lessons learned, and education. Once this dynamic knowledge is put down on paper, a static **knowledge asset (KA)** is created. The KA can be a template, white paper, code sample, or any medium that can be shared by other workers. The newly created KA is submitted to a knowledge base, or **repository,** where it is stored for use and reuse. KAs that are obtained from the base are static and contribute to the knowledge workers' growing knowledge and education. This is the simple flow of knowledge sharing that continuously raises the workers' expertise.

As an example, consider how a template is used in a consulting organization. A consultant knows that an existing cost estimation template was effectively used in the past, so she reuses it in a similar situation with a similar customer. This reuse improves the time to deliver the estimate, the accuracy of the estimate (and both reduced presale time and on-target estimates tend to result in increased profitability in the consulting business), and, in the long run, customer satisfaction. When knowledge is shared, put to practical use, remembered, and embedded in the productivity cycle, all participants in the business equation benefit:

- The enterprise benefits from increased productivity and accountability.
- Employees benefit from recognition and career growth.
- The work group benefits from shared knowledge.
- The customer benefits from productivity improvements, lower cost, and better product.
- Management benefits from improved means of accountability.
- The business (product or service) benefits from the potential for innovation.

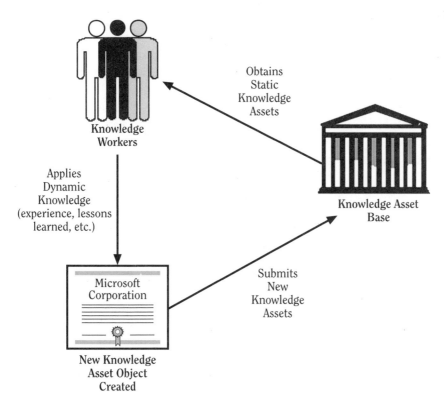

Figure 1-1.   *Knowledge Management Environment Basic Life Cycle*

The Increasing Need for Knowledge Management

KM is nothing new, of course. Managers have been trying to institutionalize organizational knowledge within enterprises for generations. Even the earliest posting of rules on the wall of a general store, such as the type of currency accepted or the return policy, can be seen as an effort to capture processes and ensure that the company's adherence to them outlives any particular employee's tenure. As companies grew, the complexity of managing and communicating knowledge grew as well. To tame this complexity, many businesses created standard operating procedure (SOP) manuals that accomplished the same goals as the rules posted in general stores, but in much more detail. An SOP manual might give the steps to shut down a nuclear reactor, for instance. However, even such large manuals could only serve as reference points to transfer the outline of organizational knowledge from one generation to another—anyone who has stepped into a new job knows that one hour with a colleague is worth a day of reading a manual.

Why is communication with a coworker so much more helpful? Because that coworker's knowledge fills in the gaps in the documentation. For example, if a new employee's job is to help assemble an aircraft carrier—a truly complicated task—reference manuals are certainly valuable and any employee would benefit from reading through the documentation. But the true KA— the knowledge of how to *apply* the information in the documentation—would still be held by workers with the hands-on experience of building an aircraft carrier. In the case of the aircraft carrier, only experienced workers could show what exactly is meant by "gentle" in the instruction "apply gentle pressure to the joystick."

The history of corporate knowledge transfer has been that of one generation of workers passing the Holy Grail of knowledge to the next. Until that time, the corporate asset—the knowledge of how, when, and what to do—was held only by the employee. In the past this process worked fine. But in today's business climate, where employees change jobs much more frequently, it becomes an issue. When workers switch jobs often, businesses cannot rely on longtime employees to transfer knowledge to others. Instead, valuable corporate assets leave the building each night with the enterprise not knowing if these assets will return in the morning. An increasingly global economy and geographically dispersed employees further complicate knowledge transfer by making face-to-face contact less common.

These changes underscore the need for enterprises to embed their organizational knowledge within the working vocabulary of every management team—and in a more permanent way. And fortunately the technology that brought us into the electronic knowledge era also offers the means to do that. KM systems capable of storing and retrieving information, and offering tools that allow presentation, search, and collaboration, have emerged to make the transformation of data and information into knowledge easier. A computer on every business desktop, instant global connectivity, collaborative tools, and cheap electronic storage provide the technical foundation to facilitate the communication required for the knowledge life cycle.

KM's Value to the Enterprise

Before we examine the processes and technology required to implement a complete KM system, it is important to reiterate the reason behind it all: value—the creation of value through collaborating and connecting knowledge sources.

The following examples of two major companies that have implemented KM systems illustrate how collaboration and knowledge sharing can benefit your organization. In a pair of reports, Giga Information Group described the environments of Bosch (the international manufacturer of automotive equipment, communications technology, consumer goods, and capital goods) and Nabisco (the international manufacturer of biscuits, snacks, and other premium food products) and explained why these world-class companies believed that collaboration and connectivity behaviors were the key success factors for them in the new economy. Knut Angstenberger, head of department Information Processing for Engineering and Sales, Bosch K5, noted that

> Accelerating time to market as a result of better collaboration amongst internal development teams and better communications with customers is a key success factor in reaching our goals for improved profitability and strengthening our international leadership position. [The system provides]... the critical collaborative headroom we require to improve document access and collaboration, thereby improving our ability to respond to market demands.[2]

The report on Bosch, from January 2001, highlighted three behaviors that Bosch sought to improve: profitability, customer satisfaction, and efficiency. The following table shows the relationship between these behaviors and the benefit to business.

---

2. Giga Information Group. "Bosch Plans Messaging Server Consolidation With Exchange 2000 Server, Anticipates Faster Time-To-Market." *http://www.microsoft.com/business/casestudies/ Bosch_E2K.asp.* (March 23, 2001).

Table 1-1.   The Relationship Between Behaviors and Benefits

Critical Success Factor	Expected Result	Business Benefit
Increase profitability	Improved agility in product development cycle.	Improved time to market.
Improve customer satisfaction	Better collaboration that accelerates time to market.	50 percent increase in reliability.
Improve business efficiency	Optional new features—online white-boarding, desktop video-conferencing, and application-sharing.	Improved productivity—5000 users each saved 1 hour per week.

Maintaining product quality while keeping up with the rapid pace of business and technology innovation is challenging for even the best companies. By providing improved customer collaboration through enabling technology, Bosch expected to reduce product development cycles and accelerate time to market, thereby sustaining its competitive advantage. The net result was projected to be both improved profits due to cost avoidance, and a strengthening of the firm's international leadership position as a premier industrial manufacturer and provider of consumer goods and services.[3]

In a similar report in March 2001, on Nabisco, Giga Information Group reported that Nabisco needed unification and seamless integration among its internal groups (people), processes, and technology infrastructure to respond to business changes and make the company an e-culture enterprise. Based on the acceptance of the KM solution by the workforce, Nabisco went into the project expecting to achieve a 2.5 percent to 4.2 percent improvement in knowledge worker productivity as a result of changing to an e-culture. Nabisco listed Microsoft's Exchange technology as one of the critical success factors in cost-effectively connecting knowledge workers and allowing seamless exchange and reuse of business information. Productivity improved due to significantly enhanced team collaboration and improved KM.[4]

What these two business case studies have in common is that both companies recognized the need to support knowledge collaboration and reuse behaviors. They both provided access to knowledge sources that were identified as critical to achieving the targeted business value. Both Bosch and Nabisco recognized that knowledge sources exist across their vast enterprises

---

3. *Ibid.*

4. "Microsoft Windows 2000 Professional and Office 2000 Fortify Nabisco's Goal of Improved Resource Utilization," as cited in Microsoft Corporation Business Value Portfolio, *Nabisco*, October 2000 & March 23, 2001. *http://www.microsoft.com/business/casestudies/nabisco-win.asp.*

in people, data sources, and valued intellectual property. The business benefit is not in recognizing or even in collecting the KAs, but in accessing and utilizing these knowledge sources.

Capturing Knowledge for Reuse

It is worth underscoring that KM is not about simply creating another database to hold explicit knowledge. It is about moving information from one person to another in a reusable format. In academic jargon, KM is the conversion of the **tacit** (the things we know and do) to the **explicit** (physical manifestation of our knowledge) and presenting the result in such a way as to encourage reuse and generate new knowledge. This is the cycle of knowledge creation. Many writers in the field of business and organizational management, including Ikujiro Nonaka and Hirotaka Takeuchi in their 1995 book *The Knowledge-Creating Company,*[5] theorize that knowledge is created in evolutionary stages:

1. Personal discovery (development of understanding based on experience)—for example, installing a software program on your computer or discovering the best way to improve plant health in a humid climate.

2. Shared understanding (producing a document, code, or other physical expression of your experiences for others to view). An example would be sharing your hypothesis on gene mapping.

3. Combining/reusing (taking shared knowledge and producing new knowledge or value through reuse or enhancement), such as utilizing lessons learned from a case study along with the original installation instructions to complete a complex software installation.

4. Researching (seeking and absorbing information in the public or semipublic arena)—for example, seeking information on printer problems from a USENET public community. In this case you might find a similar (but not identical) problem and, based on the solution proposed to that similar problem, you would figure out how to solve your unique problem.

These stages of knowledge evolution are mapped on the Knowledge Cycle diagram shown in Figure 1-2, which builds on the Knowledge Management Environment diagram from the Part I introduction. As knowledge moves from

---

5. Ikujiro Nonaka, and Hirotaka Takeuchi, *The Knowledge-Creating Company.* (New York: Oxford University Press, 1995): 74.

the Personal to the Community Space, it becomes a shared asset and is available for reuse. The broader the exposure the knowledge receives, the greater the potential for reuse and innovation.

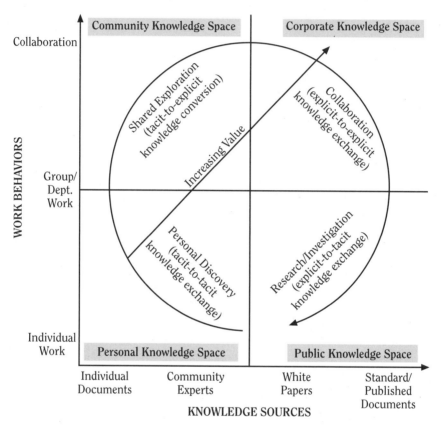

Figure 1-2. *The Knowledge Cycle and Knowledge Generation*

In the renewal or recycling of knowledge approach depicted in the Knowledge Cycle diagram, knowledge is viewed as moving from the realm of the individual through various stages of social interaction or exchange. Through this process, a social, or organizational, bridge is built that allows what an individual has learned or experienced to become part of the organizational knowledge base. To be fully utilized, knowledge must be converted from a tacit form (what an individual knows) to an explicit form (what can be viewed, reviewed, and reused by others).

Engaging Knowledge Workers in KM

KM depends on people being able to contribute their **tacit knowledge** freely and safely to others. Providing a means for people to transmit this information is as critical to KM as identifying what information is needed. If employees do not contribute to the collection of knowledge, that collection will not grow over time and it will contain limited KAs for reuse. A lack of participation will result in a shrinking, rather than growing, corporate KA base.

KM systems, along with **communities of practice (CoPs)**, make knowledge reusable. Where KM systems provide the technical framework for knowledge transfer, communities provide the organizational and cultural infrastructure for the initial steps in the knowledge creation cycle. One way to enable KM in your organization is to establish and promote communities. CoPs (also called communities of knowledge) are groups of people who share information, insight, experience, and technology in an area of common interest. Communities can operate at a workgroup, departmental, or corporate level. These groups allow contributors and users of knowledge to set their own ground rules for their exchanges. At Microsoft, for example, a group of consultants specializing in database management—even though scattered around the world—have formed a community because the members of the group share common concerns about the use of Microsoft SQL Server products. Groups of people within an organization often form informal communities around their interests and activities. If such communities do not exist or cannot be located, they can be set up specifically for their contribution to a KM system. Regardless of how communities come into existence, they are critical success factors for collaborative KM environments.

CoPs provide clarity and consensus about the type and scope of information that is available and that members want. Establishing rules for sending and receiving knowledge opens the door to collaboration. Communities establish processes for transmitting information through mechanisms such as submission templates, and for knowledge producers to receive feedback from the knowledge users or consumers. In the same way that consumers can rate a book on Amazon.com, internal knowledge consumers should be able to rate KAs in a KM system. Knowledge producers (authors or developers) need not only the declarative ratings (*outstanding, good,* or *not useful*) but also constructive feedback for improvement and recognition for contributions. Communities also help to establish a common method of exchange (language, taxonomy, unique vocabulary, and so on) that keeps the transmission moving smoothly. Providing a means to put some order in the vast array of information that can potentially be found in any repository is a significant benefit of

KM communities. Providing the appropriate structure to tag content not only by subject area but also by source (where it came from) and data type (diagram, white paper, code, and so on) or content type (a specific product or service), allows the knowledge consumer to select the information based on a broad topic or subtopic, such as a market research report. Communities are critical to the tacit exchange of knowledge because they enable person-to-person interaction and help entire groups of coworkers advance a subject area. They provide a virtual space to exchange solutions for problems, such as installing software in an unusual environment or resolving a unique design problem by sharing ideas with other designers. As a result, they create a wellspring of innovation and creative thinking at the heart of a collaborative environment.

How KM Systems Work

So how can an organization ensure the accessibility and utilization of knowledge sources within an existing environment? Let's start with a work environment that does not have a KM system in place. The group, or its management, may feel it wants to keep life simple and keep costs down by not using complex information-sharing applications. In this case they may be getting by using a combination of e-mail, file servers, and their own computers to store information. When a team member needs access to that information, that person requests it from another team member and then creates an individual copy on another hard disk or at another server location. Although fraught with inefficiencies (primarily the problem of knowing which version of which piece of information is the most current), this type of information sharing may meet the needs of this team because the team members can all participate equally and relatively quickly if the team remains small.

This basic approach can be enhanced by using a **team collaboration application (TCA)** such as Microsoft SharePoint Team Services. TCAs can make it easy for workers to track the same information on easy-to-create Web sites, conduct collaborative development efforts, and still use existing office productivity tools (such as Microsoft Word or Microsoft Excel). By carefully adding enabling technology to the existing setup, you can bring more efficiency to this type of workgroup collaboration without dampening the ad hoc nature of the information sharing. TCAs can be very basic versions of KM systems that permit small groups to collaborate, share, and store documents. However, limitations inherent in these basic systems can hamper upward scalability in the number of teams that can participate, cause security issues as the number of participants increases, or fail to support the extensive version control needed for larger organizations. TCAs are a good start on the road to KM, but they are not an enterprise solution.

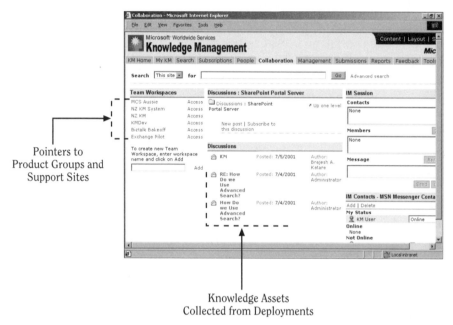

Pointers to Product Groups and Support Sites

Knowledge Assets
Collected from Deployments

Figure 1-3.   *SharePoint Sample Collaboration*

In large organizations like Bosch, Nabisco, and Microsoft, workers need information that is stored in many locations. Microsoft stores reference materials on its products in a variety of places. Product groups store code and product specific information, the support organization stores information on implementation, and the training group stores product-specific learning materials. When a consultant is called in to design a solution for a customer, he or she will often need product, training, and implementation information. If the KM solution, as shown in Figure 1-3, does not contain links, or pointers, to product group and support sites along with the KAs collected from other deployments, the consultant would lose valuable time searching these other locations for information. To centralize this information, an organization (or even divisions within the organization) can deploy central messaging services and a corporate portal to combine information from several data sources.

Broad corporate portals and collaborative systems have security and access issues that group-specific TCAs do not address. Since a corporate portal is available to the organization as a whole, security and access levels need to be set to protect company assets and to keep client and personal information from being inappropriately shared. In addition to security, the document management features of any good KM system should include versioning, routing, and publishing of content. A good content management process can provide a trusted foundation for knowledge sharing.

Corporate portals and collaborative systems (those in which the participants cooperatively work on KAs) have a symbiotic relationship. Even though a portal does not use collaborative workflow processes, it can act as an extension of the collaborative processes by providing a mechanism to present new or reinvented KAs that participants reuse. Conversely, the collaborative process reconnects the knowledge worker with the larger corporate picture through links and information-mapping techniques. Knowledge workers, communities, and the systems combine to create the KM environment within a company.

Choosing the right KM environment (the level of collaboration, connectivity, self-direction, and so on) is critical to a successful KM solution. In large organizations it may be necessary to have a mix of KM solutions to address a variety of needs. The organization may need to disseminate information (such as benefits and company news) to all employees throughout the corporation, or workgroups may need to cooperatively develop white papers, designs, or products. To produce the right solution for a given set of participants, it is important to determine the goals of your KM solution or solutions. Microsoft is a good example of a multitiered knowledge environment, with both small or limited group, as well as corporate-wide, KM needs. Microsoft has more than 2.5 million intranet pages, 2000 intranet Web sites, and 40,000 employees in more than 60 countries. It uses portal and collaborative technologies throughout the organization for department, workgroup, and corporate-wide KM needs. At the group level, a TCA solution is often appropriate, and in others a fully developed KM solution is needed to fulfill the group goals. Group-level deployments include Law & Corporate Affairs, Management IT, and Visio Launch. Information from many of these team efforts needs to be escalated upward to business unit sites or ultimately shared or published more widely on corporate sites. SharePoint Team Services allows groups this flexibility within Microsoft's environment. At the business unit level, portals such as Product Group Portal, ShowsRus, and, at the corporate level, MSWeb, operate. These projects are spread across the entire KM spectrum, but all of them use the fundamental concepts of knowledge sharing and a common technology base.

Today, the most successful collaborative systems are focused on the needs of specific business units within the organization, such as consulting, sales, or human resources, whereas portals serve the information needs of the larger audience. Microsoft adopted SharePoint Portal Server early to provide this mix of technologies for these targeted intranet sites. The company has seen a pattern in which a KM deployment in one business unit quickly leads to multiple deployments in other business units—simply said, plan well and plan early because good ideas spread quickly.

Basic Features of a KM System

KM solutions tend to be organized around immediate functional requirements. Consequently, they often end up ignoring the long-term interests of the organization, the participants, or the business. A scalable, flexible, and robust collaboration and collection solution should make it possible for participants to share and reuse information while creating a solid organizational asset base. Some of the key elements to remember as we discuss the KM solution are:

- **Storage.** The system should include a repository to put KAs. It might also have document tracking and version control, security, search, and rating capabilities.

- **Publishing.** The system should allow several people to view and access information while restricting who can create and publish the information. It might include tracking and search features.

- **Subscription.** The system should allow users to set rules regarding the information that will be automatically "pushed" to them. It might also be able to differentiate formats for certain participants, have an updating feature, and so on.

- **Reuse.** The system should provide a many-to-many publishing environment. It might include rating, restricting, and tracking features.

- **Collaboration.** The system should allow several contributors to work together to create a single piece of content and manage revision tracking. It might identify experts and their online availability, discussions, and so on.

- **Communication.** The system should capture and manage all forms of information exchange, including e-mail, phone, instant messaging, and face-to-face dialogue, and allow for spontaneous communication.

See Also   For more on KM software choices, see Part III, "The Technology of Knowledge Management." Choosing the right software is dependent upon your business drivers and goals, which are discussed in Chapters 2, "Placing a Value on Your Knowledge Management Investment," and 3, "Knowledge and the Business Culture."

Summary

Technology is the enabler of all forms of knowledge management. It allows us to include the widest possible corporate base regardless of geography and situation. It allows the knowledge-based company to collect, codify, publish, share, and innovate through the reuse of knowledge. But technology alone cannot manage knowledge for a company. As we discuss in Chapter 2, "Placing a Value on Your Knowledge Management Investment," organizations that are mobilized around KM and are guiding their efforts with appropriate KM behaviors will benefit by linking their business strategy and performance targets to their daily work. Further, as we will discuss in Chapter 3, "Knowledge and the Business Culture," the impact and power of any solution depends on how well the proposed solution is mapped to specific business processes. As we move into the definitions of metrics, organizational enablers, processes, and technology in subsequent chapters, it is important to keep the management goal of KM clearly in our line of sight.

Strategy dictates processes

Processes guide measures

Placing a Value on Your Knowledge Management Investment

This "telephone" has too many shortcomings to be seriously considered as a means of communication. The device is inherently of no value to us.

Western Union internal memo, 1876

Some people in your company might think that knowledge management (KM) is as useful to the business as a lone telephone was in 1876—an interesting device with potential but with no real defined value. Before the turn of the twentieth century, few people had telephones and even fewer people comprehended the impact of this communication device. But once the enabling technology and infrastructure were available, everyone discovered a need to communicate and it was simple to do the value equation. Today, computer technology, the Internet, and collaboration software are enabling another connectivity revolution. And just like voice communications and the telephone, the value equation is an outcome of human behaviors and activities enabled by technology.

To help people understand KM's usefulness, you have to show that it is financially worthwhile. In this chapter we will explore the role of KM in the corporate value structure, how to value KM's results, and how to link KM results to corporate profitability.

Placing a Value on Knowledge Management

In the previous chapter we learned that when information is captured and managed, it can be reused, which increases productivity and efficiency. But for financial markets and shareholders to view corporate knowledge as a source of business value, you need to find a way to measure its impact on profitability. It is critical to find a means for measuring work activities and behaviors that transform, consume, or utilize visible tangible corporate assets (such as cash or equipment) in order to provide a complete picture of a company's business value.

The problem is that most of today's accounting systems do not recognize the economic value of managing knowledge. Based on qualitative information, we know that KM helps employees reuse knowledge, but unless you can link this behavior (of knowledge reuse) to bottom-line results (by measuring knowledge flow in a company), you will not be able to measure this value quantitatively. Basing the measurement on knowledge exchange is the foundation of the knowledge-based value measurement that we will discuss in this chapter.

Accounting for Intangible Assets

Value is created when you consume, transform, produce from, or transmit a company's **assets**. Four hundred years of accounting history has taught the business world how to define and measure the performance of **tangible assets,** such as cash, equipment, and physical inventory. These assets show up on financial statements, and, with them, business managers and investors can set targets, monitor changes in the business, and compare results. But the financial models that most companies use today do not account for the return on investment of **intangible assets.** Intangible assets represent the collective knowledge, creativity, and innovative power of a company's workforce. They include the skills, experiences, data, and supporting processes that create the knowledge (understanding, writings, diagrams, and so on), services, and products of a company. A lack of tools, data, and established methods of analyzing intangible assets makes evaluating these assets a challenge.

Assessing and measuring the value of the **human capital** element of intangible assets is even more challenging than accounting for the visible types of intangibles (such as patents or data). Current accounting practices actually view activities related to human capital as an expense with no direct relationship to producing revenue. This means that only the cost—and not the value—of the work is considered. In addition, there is no residual, or future, value on the books once the work is done. This anomaly is clearly seen in the case of research work that a company purchases from an external vendor rather than using in-house labor. The cost of the purchased work may be amortized over years. But if the same work is done in house by employees, it is seen as an expense and is thus written off in the year it occurred. As a result, this employee expense is charged against current income, not the profit the research may produce. Thus, it takes away from current profitability and leaves in place the view of human capital and internal knowledge development as profit-shrinking expenses.[1]

Most, if not all, companies say that people are their most important asset. But it has been very difficult to understand, and thereby measure, the value of people (human capital). Traditional accounting's asset view, as depicted in Figure 2-1, describes just the elements, or types of assets, not how to manage and measure them. To appreciate and manage assets, we need to go beyond just listing them. Since you cannot own human capital, but only its output during the time that people work for your company, we need to look at the *effect* that human capital has on other aspects of tangible and intangible assets to understand how to determine the value that human capital has for an organization.

Asset View					
Financial (e.g. cash)	Physical (e.g. inventory)	Brand Marketing (e.g. logo)	Intellectual Property (e.g. patents)	Customers Partners (e.g. support arrangements)	Organization Infrastructure (e.g. email)
Tangible Assets		Intangible Assets			

Figure 2-1. *Accounting Asset View*

Let's compare the traditional asset view to an assets and behavioral view of accounting. In the amended view, we clarify that assets that you can physically count are "above the surface"—they are included in the financial statements, allowing business managers and investors to monitor them. But some assets are "below the surface"—these assets develop value by consuming, transforming, or producing other (physical) assets that are above the surface. "Above the surface" assets include the expected tangible assets (such as cash or equipment) that are commonly referenced on company balance sheets, as well as a subset of intangibles—those that are explicit (meaning they can be counted,

---

1. This was a concept developed by Baruch Lev in his book *Intangibles: Management, Measurement and Reporting.*

recorded or viewed) such as documents or code. The other intangibles, found "below the surface," are human assets that are assessed through their work activities and behaviors because they influence assets in tangible ways. Figure 2-2 shows the intangible behaviors—the behavioral view.

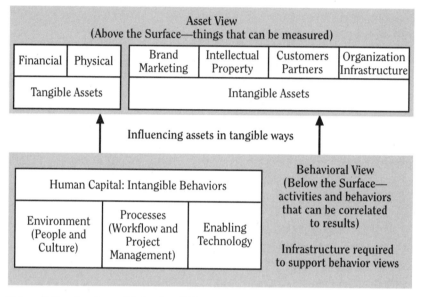

Figure 2-2.   *Assets and Behavioral View*

You can view the human capital asset value as a collection of intangible behaviors that affect the value of explicit, or visible, assets. Human capital can be monitored and managed when it performs the activities that consume, transform, or produce tangible and explicit intangible assets.

This amended view demonstrates how the intangible work behaviors people carry out (such as producing a project schedule, installing a program, or shutting down a reactor) are related to the production, transmission, and consumption of knowledge. These behaviors affect the profitability associated with tangible and more visible intangible assets, such as intellectual property and customer satisfaction. As human assets consume, transform, and produce by using these other corporate assets, they also develop new products and services—future value. If we can link work behaviors and knowledge sources (such as white papers or experts) to production, we can develop a meaningful quantitative analysis of the impact of KM on tangible and intangible assets. A measurement framework would allow us to define, measure, and link work activities, behaviors, assets, and productivity/efficiency goals, thus creating value-based KM.

A New Measurement Tool

What gets measured is valued and can be improved. If work **activities and behaviors** (the actual things people do and the ways in which that work is accomplished) and the processes that support them are not measured, the way in which they are executed and managed will not have priority and will not improve. The **KM Value Assessment (KVA) framework**, shown in Figure 2-3, is an approach you can use to understand and measure the value of effective KM in your organization. The KVA framework ties people's **activities** (things they are assigned to do), **behaviors** (how they perform the activities assigned), and performance goals (measurable targets linked to the company's strategic goals) in one view or **value chain**. The results of a KVA analysis allow a business to determine the impact of a given value chain (combination of work activities and behaviors) on profitability or production. By examining various combinations of activities-behaviors value chains, managers can more confidently guide employees in the best behaviors and processes for the current business environment. KVA can transform the vision of human capital from one of a cost to one of a revenue generator. It does this by linking work activities and behaviors to revenue-generation or revenue-supporting goals. KVA provides a method for the economic valuation of knowledge work.

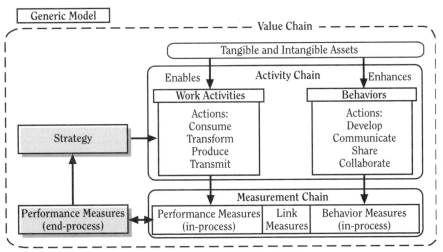

Figure 2-3.   *KVA Framework*[2]

---

2. The KVA framework was developed based on industry and academic research and practices such as the balanced scorecard, activity-based accounting, and information economics. These common measurement methods were then applied to the latest research in accounting theory on asset valuation by Professor Baruch Lev (New York University, Stern School of Management). Combining the current methods of quality and maturity measurement with the drivers presented by Professor Lev resulted in the KVA framework.

In the next section we will review each element of the KVA framework and demonstrate how it might be used in a consulting organization and a research and development (R&D) department. These examples are simple, but they will help us understand the relationships among the KVA framework's elements. At the end of this section we will close the loop back to the performance goals by correlating the activities, behaviors, and goals in the two examples.

Performance Goals

To create a benefits statement from a KVA, you need to define your performance goals along with the activities and behaviors required to support your business. As part of its business model, your organization is most likely driving toward specific measurable performance goals. Performance goals are part of one or more business strategies and should consist of measurable objectives—specific activities and deliverables that can be assigned to individuals within the company. These performance goals are both the starting and ending point of the KVA: you need to have them to determine the activities people will be performing and you need to correlate the actions people take back to the results (measured by performance of the people in terms of profitability, productivity, or efficiencies). Most businesses will have several goal statements, similar to the samples in Table 2-1. An R&D department might have the job of increasing the annual number of patents generated from research. This is a goal designed to increase the company's long-term ability to produce revenue. On the other hand, a consulting organization might have to meet current revenue targets with existing products/services. Each goal statement requires a unique KVA value chain to support it.

Table 2-1.   Performance Goals

Role	Performance Goal
R&D	10 percent growth in new patents
Consulting	Meet or exceed margin targets for all accounts

Activity Measures

A performance goal is in turn supported by or implemented through a set of services or activities within and across groups. Each activity receives a certain input, adds or modifies content, and produces a certain output. Activities are often related to (or enabled by) one or more tangible assets such as working capital, material, machinery, and tools; and intangible assets such as work by employees, information technology (use of data, computers, and so on), and organizational procedures (such as accounting or hiring procedures). You can measure the performance of each activity in terms of the cost of consumption, production, and transmission. You generally measure these work activities according to the time, effort, and other assets consumed and generated in the process of completing the work. Activities for researchers in an R&D department might include researching and analyzing specified topics. You can measure the result of their activities by counting how many white papers and patent proposals they produce. On their performance reviews, researchers are evaluated by the number (and hopefully the quality) of deliverables they produced in the review period—not by the revenue produced from the deliverables. Revenue from research is generally realized in the future. Thus, the generation of an intangible asset is the output measure of this R&D effort and the labor hours the consumption measure.

On the other hand, members of the consulting organization, in our example, are measured against current revenue and profit from activities such as needs analyses, project planning, and solution delivery to customers. The consultants are evaluated according to how they meet specific revenue goals (meeting margin) set by the management. Consultants meet these goals by delivering services to the clients through the performance of the activities listed on their performance reviews. Delivering these services quickly and well means the customer pays the service billing—and the consultant receives high marks and rewards for meeting the goals. The revenue (and possibly the customer satisfaction rating) from the deliverable is the output measure and the labor hours the consumption measure. Many of the behaviors and activities are different for the two groups, but the primary consumption measure is the same. Thus, many similar in-process measures can be associated with dissimilar performance goals.

The quality and delivery of one activity often has a cost impact on other activities. For example, poor delivery usually results in a loss of revenue or productivity. And low quality or poorly formatted information will make it harder to use the information. Searchable databases, template-based documents, or documents reviewed and edited by experts can improve quality, thus reducing the time to consume and produce information. Table 2-2 demonstrates a few sample activities we have discussed in relation to the performance goals listed earlier in Table 2-1.

Table 2-2.   Sample Activities Relating to Sample Performance Goals

Role	Performance Goal	Activities	Activity Measures (Deliverables)
R&D	10 percent growth in new patents	Researching Analyzing Recommending Implementing	White papers produced Patent proposals written
Consulting	Meet or exceed margin targets for all accounts	Gathering needs Recommending Estimating cost Reviewing Developing solutions	Needs analysis Project plans Solutions delivery

Behavior Measures

In the context of KM, we focus on the behaviors (the ways in which people work) that individuals, teams, or organizations use to reach their goals. Because these behaviors are knowledge-centric, they are highly dependent on the quality and availability of human capital (people). In the KVA framework, the work behaviors that enhance the value of corporate assets are called **behavioral indicators**. It is the behavior of an organization's people that converts tacit knowledge (solely in people's minds) to explicit knowledge (tangible enough to transfer to another worker). You can measure behavioral indicators, or the occurrences of a behavior, from a number of sources. In our R&D department example, the researchers had to research and analyze specific topics. The work behaviors related to these activities might include going to seminars, searching the company archives, or conferring with experts. In the case of the consultants, we might find them using templates for cost estimating or searching for reusable code to reduce delivery time and increase quality. You can derive information on these work-related behaviors from a number of sources, including KM systems (usage records), repositories, Web sites and portal logs, resource management, learning (records), and Human Resources (HR) systems (personnel records). You can often get data from these sources, but unless you have established methods for setting a value on the behavior's execution, how can you determine whether the behavior was the best one to use? To complicate this picture, a given activity's behavior can be different in each company. Thus, using a template may be the right behavior in a large company but wasteful in a small custom development environment. For the KVA to provide predictive behavior patterns, you need to correlate and track results over time. Mapping the behaviors executed by workers to their results will produce an initial baseline of recommended activities-behaviors sets. That is, you need to correlate the behaviors of those employees with successful delivery records to the behaviors they exhibited during the execution of their work activities to create your baseline. In the case of the R&D department example we have been looking at, you would examine the work behaviors of successful researchers (those who deliver both quality and quantity) to propose a future set of behaviors that a manager would recommend for other researchers to follow. The goal of this exercise is to produce a set of recommended activity-behavior-goal (A-B-G) combinations for managers to use in coaching their teams. These A-B-G groupings are confirmed routinely as you check the results of the KVA over time. These relationships are dynamic and will change as your business, customers, and economic factors change. Managers will need routine (quarterly or semiannual) updates on the A-B-G recommendations.

As we have emphasized, the value of human capital is based on people's ability to generate business value, measured in terms of tangible revenue, their ability to leverage other intangible assets, or both. For example, using templates in a consulting organization can reduce the cost of producing a required output, which is a revenue generator. Once the template is used, its value is buried unless the reuse (of the template) behavior is captured. The key to measuring this value is to first determine the indicators of behavior (to be measured) that would influence the generation of measurable value (work measures). In other words, how much time or money (or both) does the organization save by using this template?

When trying to define and develop indicators for measuring the value creation potential of intangible assets, there is no such thing as a "one size fits all" indicator or list of indicators. Different organizations may need to measure different behaviors in order to measure similar activities. When evaluating the appropriateness or relationship of activities and work behaviors, you should devote efforts and resources to looking at the company's people (corporate environment), processes, and technology.

Management science has demonstrated that there are common categories of behaviors in most businesses. Employee learning and growth constitutes one set of behavioral indicators present in most businesses. Our complex, knowledge-era organizations operate in an environment where customers, vendors, and suppliers often act as one virtual enterprise. Knowledge about customers, suppliers, and business partners, in this environment, is another common behavioral indicator. Value-tracking indicators that are more closely related to people include personal attributes and attitudes—these are measured by HR processes such as employee satisfaction surveys, employee retention rates, and employee productivity ratings. You can correlate specific KM measures (such as the number of new white papers submitted versus the number of white papers used) to these employee satisfaction indicators (such as employee turnover, employee absences, number of complaints per employee, number of job-related training requests, and the number of internal opportunities filled by current employees). Using these metrics could mean the difference between promoting an environment of value-creation and allowing an environment of value-destruction by dissatisfied or disenfranchised employees. Correlating these indicators with related work activities and customer-specific indicators against performance goals for profitability can provide good KM strategies.

Some correlations of HR data to KM data may validate qualitative input after increased learning (training) makes a firm more agile and able to generate business value from intangible assets such as knowledge and experience. Another qualitative statement you might validate within your organization is that the high rate of staff turnover, especially of skilled workers and knowledge workers, means a loss of valuable intellectual capital, which markets and investors agree raises the cost of capital. If these statements are true in your organization, then measuring indicators that track—and possibly counter—

such losses can become important as knowledge workers become more mobile. Motivation and empowerment in and of themselves are intangible assets. These assets are commonly measured by several things:

- the quantity and quality of employee contributions that solve internal business issues (basically measured through the number of suggestions implemented)

- team participation (quantity of team assignments in which the employee has been involved)

- the quantity and quality of the decisions made by the employee without orders from above

Similarly, intangible assets (such as a knowledge of customers and markets) are critical for creating and increasing business value. Consequently, organizations have developed KM applications to store, manage, consolidate, and share market and customer information in both structured and unstructured formats. Organizations can measure, customer by customer or segment by segment, how much business they receive. Other good activity indicators of how intangible assets contribute to create value are such variables as:

- customer retention

- customer satisfaction

- customer profitability

Table 2-3 completes our activity chain components by adding sample KM behaviors to the previously listed sample activities (in Table 2-2) and sample performance goals (in Table 2-1). KM systems can provide many noninvasive measures of behavioral indicators. You can correlate these *in situ* measures with surveys and other invasive measures for an even more comprehensive behavioral model.

Table 2-3.   Sample Behaviors Mapped to Sample Activities and Performance Goals

Role	Performance Goals	Activities	Activity Measures	Behaviors	Behavior Measures
R&D	10 percent growth in new patents	Research Analyze Recommend Implement	White papers produced Patent proposals written	Learning Knowledge asset reuse IP submission	Training (seminars) attended Templates used Best practices used/ submitted
Consulting	Meet or exceed margin targets for all accounts	Gather needs Recommend Estimate cost Review Develop solutions	Needs analysis Project plans Solution delivery	Knowledge asset reuse Learning	Templates used Best practices used/ submitted Code reuse eLearning

The Measurement Chain

The factors that influence behavior can also be measured, like any other factor, and can then be linked to performance goals. The activity and behavior measures provide the leading indicators, or in-process measurements, to achieve the desired goal, or end-process performance. Companies should monitor and manage in-process activity and behavior so that they can make decisions that maximize contribution to business performance goals. Together, these three measurements comprise a complete value chain. The KVA framework, described in Figure 2-3, provides a way to link the activities to performance goals and allows management to focus attention on those enabling behaviors that affect the activity measures. The correlation of activities to behaviors that have the desired performance result creates the measurement chain. In our consulting example we might correlate the number of code samples from the KM repository used to complete a programming assignment (work activity) to project the percentage under or over margin (delivery numbers) from the financial system. If the trend over time demonstrates that project teams exhibiting this KM behavior (that is, selecting and using code samples from the repository) consistently exceed margin, managers could advocate this behavior to their consultants as a way to meet consulting goals.

An appropriately designed interface for systems that captures and holds behavioral information is critical to developing the trending standards that make a KVA a value-based measurement of KM within a company. With solid data correlation, the KVA can reinforce beneficial behavior by prominently featuring how frequently, and to what degree, users exhibit such behaviors. Based on the data generated by the KVA, you will have developed a set of tools for illustrating the value added to the business through human capital. KVA trending also provides management with best practices for executing specific work activities. In this way the KVA also provides a method to achieve better management and accountability.

See Also   We describe the benefits and challenges of integrating these tools into a technology infrastructure in Part III, "The Technology of Knowledge Management."

Who (What Job Types) Should Be Measured?

Applying the framework for KM in evaluating work activities and behaviors, measuring the impact on business performance, or managing productivity improvement requires an understanding of when and where to do so. The first step is to define the scope of the job to be done and the activities required to do the job that could benefit from KM. KM measurement should be focused on knowledge workers and knowledge-dependent tasks that consume the majority of the workers' productive time, such as developing cost estimates, doing research, or developing processes. We need to measure activities on which knowledge workers spend a great deal of their time. These measurements help us focus on the people and performance goals that will be affected by improvements in knowledge transfer. Knowledge-dependent workers can be found throughout an organization, in groups such as R&D, regulatory and safety, information technology, and management-performing functions such as sales, marketing, and business development. Nearly all job categories in our evolving economic model are becoming knowledge-dependent. As decisions are pushed downward in nearly all industries from retail (where clerks in the retail outlet may determine when to reorder merchandise) to manufacturing (where the electrical engineer is designing a new circuit board for a airplane), knowledge, including the proper use and availability of that knowledge, is fast becoming the most important factor in productivity and efficiency improvement.

Example of a Framework in Action

A simplified example of the KVA model is given in Figure 2-4, where the example of the R&D department we have been discussing comes together. The primary activities of scientists, researchers, or other knowledge workers can be viewed as a combination of transactional activities, such as simulating a compound or running a series of tests, and work activities, such as developing a hypothesis or publishing a paper. What makes these work activities possible is primarily the experiences of individuals, organizations, industries, and academia—in other words, the efforts of the human capital and the intellectual property they bring to the job. To improve the contribution of these intangible assets, the organization needs to support behaviors that enhance the quality and quantity of these assets, such as access to a searchable database of published research; feedback from manufacturing, support, and customers; templates for writing papers; and a means for sharing ideas. We can measure both the work activities and the related behaviors. We can also measure the *impact* of behaviors on the activities. They form the in-process indicators (the behaviors and activities you measure) demonstrated in the KVA framework. These in-process measures affect the end-process or performance goal of our sample R&D group, such as getting more research done in less time. In the long term we can link the R&D performance goals to a product group and eventually to the company's performance goals. The short-term (current year) performance target for this group is to increase the number of patents by 10 percent. A simple count of the number of patents from last year with the number from this year will tell us if they achieved the goal. The real benefit for the group and its management team is to ascertain the work behaviors that helped them reach this goal. If the group measures its achievements on a quarterly basis, correlates behaviors, and tracks the results, its members can try to adjust the way that researchers approach their work in order to reach their year-end goal. In our R&D example, if the resulting trend demonstrates that people who attend less than one seminar in a quarter consistently produce fewer white papers or patent applications, or both, then management can guide researchers to attend more seminars. This is, of course, a rather simplistic example, but it demonstrates one way the KVA analysis can be used to guide a group toward success. The following diagram shows the linkages and measures for our sample R&D organization.

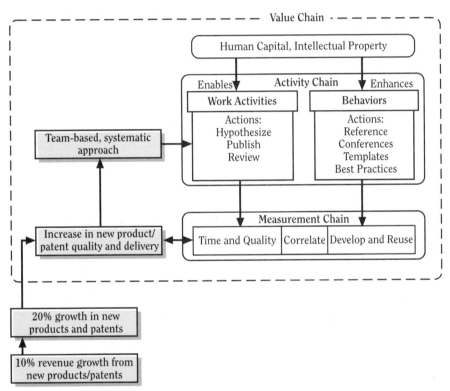

Figure 2-4. *KVA R&D Example*

We can look at other knowledge-centric roles and business functions in a similar way. Our example (shown in Figure 2-5) of the consulting group shows the performance goal to be an increase in profitability from each client engagement (contracted work). In this example, we have shown just a few of the work activities and related behaviors the consultants are charged with performing in order to complete a client engagement. In this type of service organization, assuming a fixed-price contract, time is profit. Thus, the primary measures in this case relate to time and quality of delivery. Clarity in the statement of the performance goal is critical (in this case percentage of reduction in time to delivery without loss of quality). Loosely drawn performance goals can result in incorrect results analysis and misdirection in the workplace.

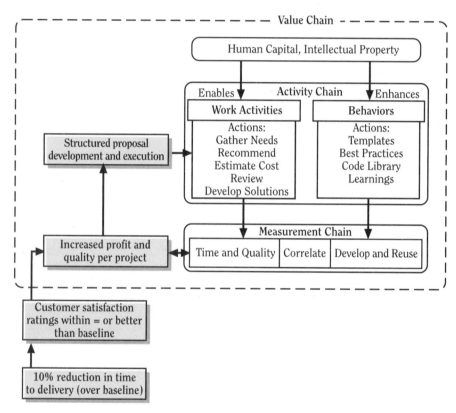

Figure 2-5.   *KVA Consulting Example*

Aligning appropriate KM behaviors (such as using templates) to work activities (such as generating proposals) should increase productivity, as well as customer and employee satisfaction (such as generating a 10 percent faster response to customer quote requests). Most companies measure work activities by using some type of performance evaluation tool. Using this information in building the KVA data framework will reduce the amount of work required to do a KM analysis. By utilizing the same activities that appear on performance reviews, quality surveys, and so on, we help employees understand the behavioral link between work performance, work behaviors, and company performance goals.

Summary

The KVA framework is designed to provide a solid and ongoing benefits analysis of KM within a business by correlating work activities and behaviors to performance goals. By linking KM measurement to the same goals used to measure individual performance (on performance reviews, for example), you align KM to the company's basic reward system and profitability. You need to compare the predicted values produced by the KVA (those derived from the analysis of trends) with actual business results to:

- Verify the value derived from the investment

- Improve the organization's ability to guide behaviors based on historical trends

- Identify activities and behaviors that do not produce the desired goals ("value blockers") and take corrective action

Apart from the benefit of knowing whether the KM investment has indeed delivered benefits, ongoing analysis also helps organizations identify factors (such as lack of use) that are blocking the realization of the benefits. In addition, ongoing analysis helps management learn which assumptions, metrics, and activities and behaviors combinations work and which do not.

KM is about how to manage better. Management and measurement are tied. If measurement does not make management better, there is no need for it. Therefore, measurement must reflect the business's goals and objectives. In essence, KM metrics are about how the organization manages its resources to achieve its goals.

Objectives dictate measures

Measures shape behaviors

Knowledge and the Business Culture

Structures of which we are unaware hold us prisoner.

Peter Senge, The Fifth Discipline

Let's say that you know your organization needs to implement a knowledge management (KM) system. But before you start evaluating technology and timelines, you should consider the degree to which KM will fit into your company culture. A company's culture is one of those intangibles that determines KM's success. The most effective KM systems make a tight fit with their company's culture, and it is those companies' employees that use KM to its fullest.

In this chapter we will explore the role of culture in KM. Then we will present a step-by-step plan for making sure your KM system is the right cultural fit for your organization.

The Role of Culture in KM

Everyone knows that business culture is real and important, but what it is and how it can be changed are less clear. Although cultural traits—style of dress, level of customer commitment, balance of work and play, attitude toward technology—might be obvious to an outsider looking in to a company, the people within the company often do not recognize them. Cultural conflicts often do not surface until someone tries to implement a new strategy or program that turns out to be incompatible with the culture. Then the power of culture becomes obvious.

In this book, **culture** refers to the interrelationships of shared history, expectations, and unwritten rules, along with the shared beliefs, behaviors, and assumptions that an organization's members acquire over time. In effect, the culture sets guidelines for what is appropriate or inappropriate for individuals (or groups), and it gives the organization cohesiveness, predictability, and stability.

The military is an example of a command and control organization with decided expectations, beliefs, and behaviors that guide its culture. The consensus management organization popular from the early 1970s through the late 1980s is at the other end of the spectrum, with a culture that thrives on compromise.

In the middle can be a whole host of dynamic organizational structures that support a variety of unique culture types. Some organizations have a casual environment and consensus management at the team level but strict top-down control of financial matters. It can be difficult to introduce change into mixed cultural environments. You may need multiple change management plans and certainly multiple communication plans.

Culture provides the context within which business is done. You can see cultural influences in the workers' day-to-day attitudes and actions—for example, a style of managing, a perspective on the customer or quality, and how employees are valued and treated. You can also detect cultural influences at the team, business unit, and organizational level, and an organization might have several subcultures. These influences are important from a KM perspective because the culture, or cultures, influence how receptive the people are to knowledge sharing and collaboration. Gaps between the culture and what is required for the desired KM program, along with worker resistance, will affect the work needed not only to implement KM, but also to get people to adopt it. For example, a management structure that does not allow enough ramp-up time to support the KM program can impede its implementation.

Although many cultural traits emerge over time, you can proactively deploy and support specific beliefs, behaviors, and assumptions that will support your strategic objectives. In other words, you plan and implement certain cultural traits that will improve your chances of achieving success as defined by management. For instance, an organization might decide that, in order for KM to succeed, it should move toward a more collaborative, sharing environment, but its culture might be oriented toward the individual (rewarding the individual over teamwork). You can, however, change this culture to make it more collaborative. This change would require several things:

- A clear statement of the desired way of operating

- Identification of the organizational processes and systems (such as goal-setting and performance evaluation) that need to be changed to bring about the desired assumptions, behaviors, and beliefs

- A plan for communicating the new approach and for shifting the organization's systems

Shifting a culture is not easy, and many organizations underestimate the difficulty of designing a cultural shift.

The key point is that all organizational cultures can have KM philosophies and activities, but the strategy, approaches, and organizational investments they use will vary depending on the culture fit. In some cases an understanding of culture may result in a KM program specifically designed to fit in that context. In other cases the desired KM program and employee behaviors may drive significant cultural changes that affect the way people think and work. In other words, implementing a KM program itself may cause cultural change.

Fitting KM into Your Culture

Culture can make or break a KM initiative. If the KM program or initiative does not fit into the existing culture, resistance can emerge at the individual, group, and organizational levels. Even the best-planned programs are at risk if you do not pay attention to this strong, and often overlooked, force.

The good news is that you can assess your organization's culture *before* implementing a new KM solution. The steps to do that are:

1. Define your business strategy for the culture.

2. Define the culture you want to create.

3. Identify gaps between the current culture and the desired culture.

4. Close the gaps with culture change. This change can involve both "soft" (people-oriented) and "hard" (systems-oriented) solutions.

5. Develop an integrated plan.

6. Monitor the results.

Organizational culture orients every employee's attitude and actions. Consequently, it is important to have a clear understanding of your culture, develop a solid plan of action for your KM solution, and monitor the results. The rest of this chapter will address each of the steps in detail.

Step 1: Define Your Business Strategy

Even before you start looking at your organization's cultural status quo, you have to define (or remind yourself of) the overall business strategy. Your strategy affects your decisions on whether you adapt KM to your culture, whether you change the culture to adapt to a KM model, or whether you do a combination of both.

In general, a critical success factor for KM is a clear linkage to the overall business strategy. From the start, you have to make this strategy decision based on the overall business or competitive strategy, specific business problems or opportunities, and the type of knowledge that needs to be shared and used. Without this, KM is peripheral to the real business and potential benefits will not be fully realized.

Only after you understand the strategy and objectives can you select appropriate KM approaches to support them. Although one company may benefit most from a large document repository and investments in content management, others may do better with an emphasis on collaboration and ways to connect people across diverse groups and regions. Consulting is an excellent example of the latter. Whereas some firms, particularly those offering highly customized strategy services, will invest in collaboration processes, enabling technologies, and organizational policies, others that emphasize reusable knowledge will invest in repositories, processes, and organizational policies to reinforce those desired behaviors. A good illustration of a repository or library approach to KM is Microsoft's public Web site, *http://www.microsoft.com* or an internal human resources Web site, where users can view, read, and copy product, service, and company information from the Web site. This approach results in a storehouse of quality information that is shared. A collaborative approach, on the other hand, is one where the users of the KM system actually contribute information and communicate with one another. A consulting firm would use a collaborative KM system to share workflows and best practices (proven procedures) by industry experts. A collaborative environment might support a common workflow process to develop documents or share lessons learned from customer projects. Your choice of repository or collaborative system affects how you will design strategies and make investments in KM (and, eventually, the results). For example, you cannot expect to get collaborative behaviors or an instant knowledge-sharing culture if your investment strategy revolves around technology-enabled document repositories designed for viewing published material. But if your goal is a large library system for best practices, this may well be the best solution.

Once you define your business strategy, you must review and analyze your company culture and organization. This understanding gives you a baseline and helps you predict what receptivity or resistance you may meet by implementing a KM program. For example, if you determine that you need a collaborative culture to meet business objectives but the culture has traditionally been one that encourages and rewards individual contribution, the chance of success without change and redirection is small. Generally speaking, the bigger the gap or change, the bigger the investment you need to make in culture fit and realignment.

Step 2: Identify the Desired Culture

Once you have determined your organization's business strategy, your next step is to determine what the organization and culture should look like to meet these goals. To do this, ask what is *needed* for the KM solution to achieve maximum benefits. Consider the culture and organization elements that will need to be in place to support the change or the new KM program. How would a KM solution affect employees? What new behaviors are required? How big or small are the changes? What can you do to prepare the organization and people for these changes? The statement of your current operations and how you envision the "new" environment (to support KM) will let you conduct a gap analysis.

As an aid in this process, picture the Knowledge Cycle as shown in Figure 3-1. Ask what needs to be stored. What knowledge is critical to your business in each quadrant? Who needs to produce that knowledge (who are the knowledge sources)? Then focus on knowledge consumption or use (work behaviors) and consider where a natural fit exists. Keep in mind how knowledge is naturally created and evolved (as depicted in the Knowledge Cycle). Then determine the quadrants your company wants its knowledge to reside in and what it will take from a cultural adoption perspective to get there.

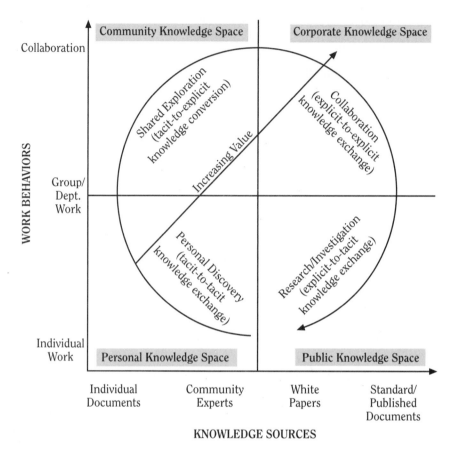

Figure 3-1. *Knowledge Cycle with Activity Sources*

For example, if your company's culture is currently "hero-based" and tends to be autocratic with employees, you could implement a KM program that fits into that structure—one with fewer communities and limited collaboration approaches. Or you could prefer that your company change to have a more sharing and collaborative culture. In that case, not only would you design a different KM program, but you would also have to do much more work in the areas of organizational and cultural change (such as changing the reward structure and instituting teaming). KM strategy must be aligned to company culture to achieve success.

Step 3: Identify Gaps

The next step is to conduct a **gap analysis**. A gap analysis spells out the difference between the current state and the desired state (desired state – current state = gaps). The key differences between the two states are considered gaps that need to be closed. For example, if you determine that people need to start sharing information such as successful sales proposals, yet the performance rewards give bonuses based on individual sales, there is a gap. To allow for the sharing of sales proposals, you must first eliminate or alter the reward for individuals to also include team rewards. More difficult to address are subtleties like entrepreneurial or innovative cultures that value creativity over building on what was already been done. These can be some of the hardest barriers to overcome when working toward a true knowledge-sharing culture.

Step 4: Closing the Gaps with Culture Change

The goal of a gap analysis is to identify and prioritize areas in which there are large gaps between the current organization and culture and the desired one. These gaps are a major barrier to implementing change, so addressing the affected areas is a substantial step toward achieving the goals of the KM implementation on time and within budget. Once you have identified the gaps, you have a few choices:

- **Modify the culture.** In some cases, a new KM plan is *designed* to change the underlying structure of how people think and behave. In these cases, it is important to take the strength of the culture into account when you plan the change and ensure that the leaders of the change are aware of the level of commitment and resolve they will need to overcome the inertia created by the current culture. Leaders of change vary depending on the organization; in some cases they are management and in other cases they are empowered employees. In addition, it may be desirable to phase the change in, or to pilot it in areas where it is likely to receive higher acceptance, gaining momentum that can be used to overcome the cultural barriers in other parts of the organization.

- **Modify the change that is required.** In other cases, the aspects of the new solution that opposes the current culture may not be critical to deploying a successful solution. In these situations, it is generally best to shape the solution to the culture as much as possible, allowing for a more rapid and successful implementation process. Find a way to break the change down into smaller chunks, to slow down its implementation in this part of the organization, or to pilot it in particularly receptive areas to gain some momentum. For example, you might recruit a community member to give presentations explaining the change and its benefits to small groups of workers.

- **Prepare for the long road.**   If sponsors are unwilling to change the initiative or resources and expectations, it is likely that the KM plan will initially fail to meet its objectives in this part of the organization. The implementation team can help prepare for this possibility by making contingency plans and helping the organization recognize and mitigate the risks associated with a failure to fully implement the change.

Once your gap analysis is complete, make a comprehensive list of the issues that you need to address and the recommended solutions. Identify any issues that are already being addressed in some way (perhaps through other organizational initiatives). Bring the remainder of the list to the attention of decision-makers in the organization so that you can modify the KM proposal or make other decisions about addressing these risks.

Making Cultural Changes

A critical success factor for a KM initiative is that it is recognized and managed. KM generally brings some organizational and cultural changes; it is the scale and scope that vary from organization to organization.

When KM philosophies and activities are introduced, individuals and groups might need to operate in ways that differ from the familiar patterns of the current culture. Changes that depart dramatically from the current culture are called **countercultural changes**. Because culture is an extremely strong force for stability, countercultural changes often fail.

When a new business strategy or process is introduced, culture can come into play in three ways during its implementation:

- First is the degree of consistency between the requirements of the new process and the culture that exists in the organization. Because culture is so powerful, a change that appears to violate current ways of thinking or behaving will be very difficult to make. On the other hand, a change that people see as aligned with current habits and ways of thinking will be easier to complete.

- The second way culture may play an important role during the implementation of a new process is by its overall strength. A culture's strength can either help or hinder a change.

- The third aspect of culture that can play a role in change involves past transitions. People base their beliefs, behaviors, and assumptions about what will happen when a new change is announced on their prior experiences with change. If previous changes were well implemented, the culture generally supports new changes. If previous changes were poorly implemented, people might be wary of new changes.

Understanding these issues and how they affect personal and organizational reactions to change can help people at all levels make sense out of what they see going on around them during a major change.

The Starting Point

Human behavior, like many other things in the world, is subject to inertia. It tends to settle into a stable state. Overcoming the tendency to retreat to what is familiar requires a great deal of motivation.

Taking the initial step to change has several fundamental requirements. There must be a force that starts the process and several additional components that lead to sustained progress. One obvious source of motivation for change is a new solution. But although an attractive and accessible solution might set change in motion, it probably will not sustain it through the ambiguity of transition.

Three other elements must be in place if the movement is to be maintained:

- A high level of discomfort with the situation that exists before the change. This will make it less likely that people will seek to return to the earlier state.

- A good plan to achieve the desired state through implementation of the solution. Without this plan, the ambiguity during transition may be overwhelming, leading to frustration and confusion.

- A clear picture of the desired end state. This enables people to share a vision of the goal they are all pursuing.

Recognizing this process and its key elements allows individuals to see where they are in the flow of events, to identify any missing elements in their own and others' motivation to change, and to intervene in the process to produce change.

Methods to Facilitate Change

The previous section emphasized that an organizational or cultural change gains initial momentum when there is a compelling solution, dissatisfaction with the status quo, a good plan, and a clear vision of the future. Building on this, when you contemplate the task of changing an organization's culture or aligning an organization to support and reinforce a new program such as KM, it is helpful to consider two aspects that, when managed holistically, greatly increase the likelihood of success: aligning with business strategy and aligning with people.

As discussed earlier, an understanding of and alignment with the overall business strategy is the first step toward making the organizational and cultural changes that a KM program needs. From a leadership perspective, the program must be grounded in business objectives and must support the organization's overall goals. With this comes leadership support and sponsorship, which are required for any significant change that requires the organization and the people within it to move from the status quo to a new state. Leadership then articulates and promotes the business case and value to the organization and individuals. Here is where the momentum starts and key questions are answered, including

- Why are we changing?
- Where are we going?
- What is the plan for getting there?

Once you define the details of the new KM program, it is time to evaluate and plan for its impact on the organization. A new KM strategy must map to the way people work and are organized within your company. The following is a checklist of the major issues to consider when you align your KM strategy with your company's culture.

❑ **Define strategy and alignment.**   Effective KM is both tactical (the way users share/leverage knowledge) and strategic (the way KM activities solve real business problems and impact the bottom line). The key value of business and strategy alignment is the ability to link KM activities to business objectives and measures.

❑ **Align business processes.**   To be effective, KM needs to be grounded in the typical user's business processes, and KM activities need to be integrated into the user's daily life and work activities. When business processes are aligned with the KM plan, there is a greater chance that the new system will be used.

❑ **Obtain leadership and sponsorship.**   Leadership and sponsorship are critical to the success of the new KM plan. Not only do leaders need to promote KM, but they must also approve the organizational changes and resources required to reinforce the new way of working. The key value of leadership and sponsorship is top-down commitment to the value of the effort and of time and resources.

❑ **Align the organizational structure.**   When considering a change to work processes or activities that people do, it is important to consider whether the current organizational structure facilitates or hinders the new way of working. The key value of organizational structure is the alignment of the environment in which workers operate with the KM goals, processes, and system.

❑ **Align the people infrastructure.**   The KM solution will require an infrastructure and resources to maintain the system, including environment (people and culture), process, and technology components. You must put people resources in place to sustain the KM system and activities. Consider the number of people required, the KM roles and skill sets required, and whether or not pure KM roles or KM activities are integrated into existing roles. (See Chapter 5, "Creating and Sustaining Communities of Practice," for more details on KM roles.)

❑ **Align performance management—develop rewards and incentives.**   What is measured is what gets done. If an organization wants people to participate in knowledge-sharing activities and use the systems and tools, the performance management system must reinforce the desired behavior. This includes both informal and formal rewards and recognition, as well as incentives that support KM goals. It is more than simply adding a new measure to a scorecard. It is about communicating what is important and valued in the company and then backing that up with actions.

❑ **Develop and implement KM education.**   Moving toward a knowledge-sharing environment requires formal and informal education to ensure that people understand what KM is about, the business case and value, the vision, and the way KM helps the company and employees profit. Additionally, you will need to implement some formal training activities, such as KM orientation, training for KM roles, and instructions on how to use the system.

❑ **Communicate and evangelize KM.**   Communication is critical throughout the project to set initial expectations, business case, and vision, to distribute key information about strategy and action plans, to keep people informed on progress and changes, to solicit feedback, and to share and celebrate successes. The key value of communication is the actual sharing of important information and setting expectations—moving people along the communication continuum from simple awareness, to understanding, to acceptance, and ultimately to internalization—and simply filling the information void so that people do not fill the void themselves—a primary cause of resistance to change.

❑ **Develop KM metrics and measurements.**   KM must have both process and outcome measures to be successful. Process measures track KM-specific activities such as submitting IP to a repository or joining a community. Outcome measures move to actual business value measures and are often linked to business processes and return on investment (ROI). Typically, the first measures represent the baseline and, over time, outcome measures are integrated. The key value of metrics and measures is that KM activities are tracked and linked to business outcomes. This increases the likelihood that KM activities will be supported throughout the organization and gets closer to the elusive ROI measures and intangible asset valuation.

Although it may surprise many people, a well-constructed, logical business strategy aligned to a new solution or program still may not be welcomed and adopted with excitement. This is where the subtle culture barriers and individual resistance emerge. Thus it is critical to focus on activities that decrease resistance to, and increase acceptance of, the change. Carefully using communication to inform and move people from awareness to acceptance and finally adoption is a place to start. One option might be to create small focus groups to help communicate the positive side of the change to help manage its impact. For example, in an effort to realign its communities of practice, the first step for Microsoft Consulting Services (MCS) was to confirm that community members understood and agreed that the business and products were changing. Once the focus groups and field surveys confirmed that they had the right direction, the new structures were designed. Providing opportunities for participation and for sharing concerns is important to influencing cultures and implementing change in organizations.

Understanding Resilience

Resilience—the ability to absorb disruptive change while maintaining productivity and quality standards—is essential to successful change. Perhaps the central issue in demystifying change is the recognition that individuals can only absorb change that they understand and that some people are better able to do this than others. Once people understand that they can change and that they can further develop their abilities (skills and experiences), they tend to support the change rather than create resistance to it. Resistance is a natural part of change. People's emotional reactions to change are often predictable. This predictability is based on their initial favorable or unfavorable perceptions of a change. Those who initially perceive the change favorably react very differently from those who see the same change as unfavorable from the beginning. Once you understand each of these reactions, you can help people to better anticipate their own and others' resistance and to develop strategies for dealing with it.

Commitment is the source of energy that propels people and organizations through the change process. Commitment is not a yes-or-no issue. When making a change, people move through a series of stages, ranging from initial contact to treating the changed way of operating as the new status quo. Furthermore, their intellectual and emotional engagement with change may proceed at different speeds. When people understand the process of commitment, they can recognize their own and others' commitment levels, provide information to guide people to the next step of the process, and recognize the costs and benefits of achieving various levels of commitment.

Step 5: Develop an Integrated KM Plan

Although you must define a plan that identifies, prioritizes, and addresses cultural gaps, these efforts cannot operate in isolation. The fastest way to undermine the implementation of a KM program is to consider the changes that need to be made in the people and culture as peripheral activities that are separate from the actual solution. You cannot make organizational and cultural changes upfront or, as often occurs, at the end of the implementation. These changes must be evolutionary and take place alongside the definition and implementation of the KM solution. Ideally, you will create a master plan that addresses the overall KM solution, including technology, people/organization, and process aspects. You plan and implement them in a holistic way, as each is dependent on the other. The processes, discussed in Part II, "The Process of Knowledge Management," are guided by the structure that is permissible in the corporate culture and required by the business goals. The technology architecture and design, discussed in Part III, "The Technology of Knowledge Management," depend on the business rules that are dictated by the corporate culture and business goals discussed here.

Step 6: Monitor Results

You might think that once the new KM solution or change is implemented, the work is over. This is far from the truth. In addition to general evaluation activities, it is also important to monitor ongoing culture alignment with KM solutions, as well as people's perceptions of the value and effectiveness of the KM solutions. One way to do this is through annual culture checks.

Many organizations conduct employee polls; some make it an annual event, others do a quarterly review, and others use focus groups. However it is done, an employee poll is an opportunity to measure KM-related attitudes, such as whether employees believe they are rewarded and recognized for knowledge sharing, whether they believe they are accountable for knowledge sharing, and whether they believe they have the information and knowledge they need to do their job. This culture check-in is a good way to measure receptivity to a knowledge environment. If a program has been put in place, it is a good way to understand whether attitude or behavioral changes have been adopted. For example, consider adding poll questions such as "am I accountable for sharing information and knowledge outside my workgroup?" and "am I rewarded for sharing information and knowledge outside my workgroup?"

Summary

Even the best-planned KM program implementations are at risk if you do not pay attention to the organization's business culture and business goals. To ensure that the desired KM solution fits your organization, take time to go through the steps of discovery—define the current culture and your business strategy, identify the desired culture, identify gaps between the current culture and the desired culture, close the gaps, develop an integrated plan, and, above all, monitor results. Following these six steps will help lower the risks during and after your KM implementation. With the KM foundation now built, it is time to move to the basic construction of what your KM solution will look like. Part II will direct you through the building processes.

Culture drives behavior

Behavior produces results

The Process of Knowledge Management

A desk is a dangerous place from which to view the world.

John Le Carré, British novelist[1]

When you implement a knowledge management (KM) system in your organization, a holistic, multidisciplinary approach is vital to ensure success. It is important to look at how the solution will be used in the organization. As we have mentioned before, you cannot just buy a successful KM solution off the shelf—environment, processes, and technology are all part of a solution. Before you can implement KM, you need to understand its intangibles: the goals of a knowledge-based organization, the management process, and the technology environment for KM. Just as Part I explained strategy and environment in value-based KM, Part II presents a clear picture of the processes required for a KM implementation. These are the building blocks of KM on which any discussion of tools and technologies (which we address in Part III) is founded.

In the next four chapters we will focus on ways to implement KM strategic and tactical goals within an existing or evolving organizational structure. Key to this discussion is gaining a clear understanding of the alignment of knowledge goals, work behaviors, and the sources of knowledge, as shown in Figure II-1. It is important to understand what knowledge should be visible and how it will be used and managed throughout the Knowledge Cycle. In each quadrant of the Knowledge Cycle, the way knowledge is developed and created is different. As stated in Part I, all knowledge starts as personal knowing (or know-how) and is shaped by the individual into a tangible (or

---

1. From *The Honourable Schoolboy.*

explicit) shareable asset. Often knowledge created in the Personal Space is published directly to the corporate or Public Space without becoming an asset in a smaller community (such as a community of practice or interest). To build or buy the right KM solution for a company, it is critical to understand not only the company culture but also that knowledge is first and foremost an asset of the individuals who convert what is known (tacit) into storable, shareable knowledge that can form the basis of new knowledge—and innovation. If the company culture rewards and supports this type of teamwork, individuals will contribute to the knowledge base; if the company rewards and promotes only individual successes, then no matter how good the KM technology enablers are, the knowledge base will not contain the best or the most critical information to foster innovation.

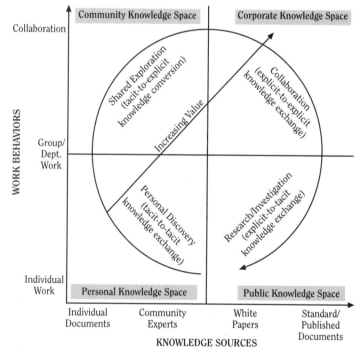

Figure II-1.   *The Knowledge Cycle*

Organization of This Section

Throughout this section you will find tips and techniques not only for institutionalizing KM but also for supporting a knowledge-based organization. Chapter 4, "An Implementation Framework," gives an overview of the stages of KM implementation, from knowledge creation to knowledge reuse. It also tackles the difficult questions of cost and risk inherent in any KM solution.

In Part II we address the building blocks that are universal to good KM solutions. Chapter 5, "Creating and Sustaining Communities of Practice," describes communities of practice which are groups of employees with a common interest. You can make use of these communities of practice to help you find and reuse knowledge in your organization. Chapter 6, "Building Taxonomies," shows how taxonomies, or commonly understood classifications of products, services, or information, can help you streamline the ability to find (search for) knowledge in your KM solution. Finally, Chapter 7, "Capturing Your Organization's Knowledge Assets," delves into how you can tap the knowledge within your organization by collecting and managing knowledge assets.

An Implementation Framework

If no one ever took risks, Michelangelo would have painted the Sistine floor.

Neil Simon, American playwright

For **value-based knowledge management** to be a success in your organization, you need to carefully consider how to implement your knowledge management (KM) solution. This chapter introduces the fundamentals of implementation—preparing and organizing your environment for KM. KM solutions range from one-way corporate information portals to highly collaborative environments. Regardless of the scope or technology of your KM solution, the solutions to problems of knowledge creation, capture, organization, storage, and distribution have similar characteristics.

Once you have clarified the basic functions that your organization's KM solution will fulfill, you should recognize the solution's costs and risks. Planning for implementation will require you to anticipate the what-ifs as well. In the second half of this chapter we will explore the costs and risks and discuss how to prepare for them.

Starting to Implement a KM Solution

Regardless of the scope and scale of a KM initiative, it includes key functions that leverage explicit knowledge for the benefit of an intended audience. These key areas form the basis for making and using knowledge assets (KAs) in KM. The degree to which you adopt these functions depends on your choice of KM systems, but regardless of which KM system you choose, you will want to address each of these issues:

1. Creating knowledge

2. Capturing knowledge

3. Organizing knowledge

4. Sharing and distributing knowledge

5. Using and reusing knowledge

As Figure 4-1 shows, the Community, Corporate, and Public Spaces can contribute to the capture, organization, and distribution of created explicit KAs. Specific participation of these groups depends on the intended audience for the KA.

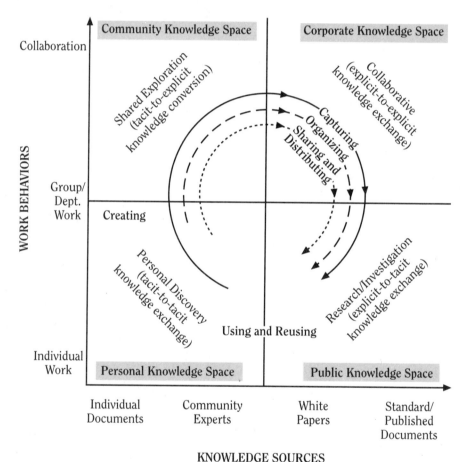

Figure 4-1. *The Knowledge Cycle and Knowledge Assets*

In this figure we added the five functions to the familiar Knowledge Cycle to illustrate how the functions are distributed in KM. Knowledge creation, distribution, and reuse do not necessarily take place consecutively. We see that creating begins in the Personal Knowledge Space; sharing and distributing, organizing, and capturing begin in the Community Knowledge Space—and sometimes continue to the Corporate Knowledge Space and end in the Public Knowledge Space. To understand the Knowledge Cycle, let's take a look at a KA that the author of this book recently created. I wrote a white paper called "Valuing Knowledge Management Behaviors" in my Personal Space (on my local PC) using knowledge collected from both public and corporate sources. After the World Congress on Intellectual Capital approved the paper, it was distributed in the Corporate Space in prepublication format. Finally, the paper was published in the Public Space, completing the Knowledge Cycle.

When an organization moves through these five functions as part of a KM solution, it has an organized system for creating, publishing, and using (or reusing) the most significant information and explicit business knowledge. The organization will be able to capture what it needs for its current business objectives, and it will reduce redundancy and duplication efforts. The five functions ensure that employees are most likely to find the information they need and will not waste time learning new ways of looking for information. They also ensure that once employees are ready to share what they know, they can reach those who need to know it. Ultimately, this process results in measurable benefits through reuse and informed decision-making.

Function 1: Creating Knowledge

The goal of any KM program is to link its tacit knowledge to other people and other generations of employees. The act of knowledge creation is dynamic and includes what individuals possess through their experiences, learning, and talents—all this forms the basis of tacit knowledge. Once it is expressed in any form (such as words, pictures, and sounds), the knowledge becomes static and explicit. If, for example, after reviewing the workflow for invoice processing within your organization, you develop a new process, your creation remains a dynamic one until you write it down. This is the key to knowledge generation and innovation in an organization. You have come up with a solution to a problem and have moved knowledge from the dynamic state to the static state, thus becoming an **author** of new ideas.

The Culture of Knowledge Creation

The more your employees contribute their knowledge to your KM solution, the more useful the solution will be. You can increase your employees' participation in this authorship process by motivating them. Depending on your organization's culture and its attitude toward information sharing, you can choose to motivate with reward and recognition programs, performance management expectations, or tightly drawn business processes. If an employee comes up with an idea to solve a particular problem in the group, a committee can be formed to collaboratively discuss and come up with even more solutions to the problem. If your organization's author participation is low, you can either change the culture to improve it or change the infrastructure to make participating easier. For example, if you require knowledge workers to become authors, allocate time in the schedule so that authoring is a priority. The more empowered an employee feels to publish authored materials, the more likely he or she will do it. Knowledge workers feel empowered when they know that, come performance review time, they will be rewarded for innovating and creating content.

Editors in the Creation Function

In most KM systems, almost anyone can be an author—that is, almost anyone can write or create a piece of information that is to be included in the database of knowledge that an organization keeps. But a good KM system also needs **editors** who select specific content for an intended audience. The person in that position might ensure that messages are consistent, ensure that the most significant content is brought to the audience's attention, and direct the audience to important events in the business process. An editor in a sales organization ensures that announcements and sales promotion messages are consistent with what the product group has developed. How formal or informal the editorial process is depends on the audience. Formal structures, such as Microsoft's public Web site, *http://www.microsoft.com*, may require trained journalists to write and edit knowledge for the intended audience. In collaboration-centric internal structures, such as internal Web sites, this role is best handled by a subject matter expert who is highly regarded by his or her peers. The subject matter expert also serves to motivate others in the group to contribute. Some organizations need someone who just checks for content quality to ensure that the most relevant information and knowledge are made available.

Function 2: Capturing Knowledge

Capturing knowledge is the process of identifying business-related information or static knowledge that supports and builds the organization's asset value. In our discussion on the authoring process, we mentioned the need to address the audience as well as the needs of the business. In KM environments, it is important to organize the repository (library of business knowledge) so that potential authors understand what the knowledge consumers' needs are and how they can meet those needs with knowledge creation. For example, virtual communities (of practice or interest) that are common enablers of KM within companies often provide structures that list the knowledge their participants want from experts, in the form of knowledge asset indexes or request lists, for example. In Web sites such as USENET communities (see *http://communities.microsoft.com/newsgroups/default.asp?icp= windowsXP* as an example), knowledge consumers post questions requesting knowledge from experts. To ensure reuse and value, you should not consider the creation process complete until the author identifies how the information fits into the overall organizational structure. Mapping, indexing, and requesting mechanisms are only some of the methods used to make knowledge accessible to the end user; tagging KAs as they are contributed is another accessibility tool. Most KM software systems support tagging in some form. Accurate and specific classification helps make searching and retrieval fast and fruitful for the user. If, for example, you tag content that defines and describes Microsoft Windows XP, it is important to make sure that the tag reads *Windows XP* with a space between the word *Windows* and before the *X* in *XP*, not *WindowsXP* or any other combination. Otherwise, a user's search will not bring up everything in the repository on the subject.

Information is multiplying at an extreme rate. Microsoft, as just one corporate example, has well over 2000 intranet Web sites, over 2.5 million Web pages, and endless amounts of data shared through distribution lists and e-mail and stored on file shares, on hard disks, and in public folders. Within this intensive information environment, numerous corporate-wide initiatives focus on ensuring the capture of corporate knowledge of value within the company. With so many diverse subjects within the corporation, tagging explicit content or indexing it, or both, makes it possible to search through the 2000 intranet sites and retrieve the correct knowledge assets.

Function 3: Organizing Knowledge

If information is to be useful to others, it needs to be more than just collected. It needs to be organized according to the business rules that relate to the structure and use of KAs. Otherwise, others will not be able to find and reuse that information. Information that is classified and mapped to other knowledge is more likely to be reused because it is easier to locate. An organization system can help ensure that the information you create and capture is distributed and reused.

Your organization needs to decide on how information will be structured and what technology will be used to access it:

- when employees use e-mail
- when they use public folders
- when they use a team site
- when they use a departmental portal

Also, can employees decide when to use each vehicle, or will you mandate a certain use? If it is up to employees, individuals and groups can initiate grassroots practices with e-mail aliases or team sites. If your organization will mandate a certain use, you will need to establish policies on accessibility, security, and appropriate use of vehicles for corporate messaging, information related to strategic initiatives, access points to repositories of corporate know-how, and planning.

Establishing a taxonomy (both of a way to retrieve content and of the information and knowledge itself) is critical. A taxonomy ensures that employees don't find redundant information or spend endless hours searching for information across myriad search environments. If the taxonomy is done right, it should lead the individual to the most authoritative sources of information and knowledge in a direct, obvious way. Employees can then spend less time looking for, and more time using, the information and knowledge. This process also helps to ensure that the best available information and knowledge is used for decision-making. Clarity in, and organization of, information storage make a huge difference in empowering employees to do their best work and spend more time using what they need instead of looking for it.

See Also   We explore taxomonies in more detail in Chapter 6, "Building Taxomomies."

Function 4: Sharing and Distributing Knowledge

Sharing and distributing knowledge means making knowledge available to others. It starts with ensuring that the people in an organization are motivated to share their knowledge in the first place. How much knowledge is shared depends on an organization's culture. If the organization values individual excellence over team excellence, there may be less motivation to share information and knowledge. If the organization rewards results, regardless of how they are documented for future benefit, there likely is less motivation to publish. If an organization does not invest in the tools and applications that make it easy to share, employees will be less willing to do so. If an organization is hierarchical and there is a grassroots initiative to increase knowledge sharing, there is little likelihood that others will share their knowledge outside the grassroots team, even if it is important to a broader audience.

See Also   For an in-depth discussion of:

- how culture impacts KM, see Chapter 3, "Knowledge and the Business Culture."

- rewards and recognitions, see Chapter 5, "Creating and Sustaining Communities of Practice."

You can put several systems and processes into place that encourage greater levels of sharing. You might have leaders sponsor and communicate sharing initiatives. You could also find technology solutions that make sharing easier. To determine how well your organization shares knowledge, consider your answers to the following questions:

- How many times was work redone because it was impossible to find the previous files or even the individuals with know-how?

- How hard is it for your organization to find the information and knowledge it needs to do the job?

- How many times were experts hired and their work lost due to the lack of a system that could capture their work regardless of who they were doing it for?

Knowledge sharing can help you avoid these types of information gaps that are costly to the organization.

See Also   Chapter 5 continues this discussion with an in-depth look at structuring KM environments and knowledge communities.

Distributing knowledge well depends on the channels of distribution that the target audience uses and on the channels' effectiveness. When a business's work is predominately conducted face-to-face, distributing knowledge is most effective during one-on-one or group meetings where both tacit and explicit knowledge is exchanged. Consider the case of a software development group that is required to design a new version of a product. Its members have the explicit knowledge of the old product, and they all have tacit knowledge (ideas based on their experiences) of the changes they want to make in the new version. Once the new features are written into a new functional specification, the team emerges with a new set of explicit knowledge. In most fast-paced organizations, this knowledge exchange is an essential element of the development process.

Technology enables distribution, either through knowledge repositories that are accessed through Web interfaces and public folders or shared through distribution lists. Knowledge distribution can be passive—for example, an online library containing books and articles of information where workers can go to download information, requiring the target audience to seek the knowledge and extract what they need. Or knowledge distribution can be active; an online newsletter mailed to subscribers is a good example of pushing information and knowledge to a target audience based on user subscriptions to the content or based on an organization's determination that a specific audience needs the information. The distribution method you choose depends on your organization's structure and your workers' needs. Some organizations are e-mail-centric, others are Web-centric, and others may choose specifically when to use either of these methods. A typical scenario in a knowledge-based environment is one in which workers use the Web more frequently for corporate communications but use e-mail for exchanging knowledge with peers. KM solutions will tend to direct and organize these distribution approaches. Personalization and subscription services, as described in Part III, "The Technology of Knowledge Management," add a "push" dimension to knowledge distribution. Subscription services require a strong commitment by the organization to publication methods, including taxonomies and knowledge structures (such as indexes, which are described in Chapter 7, "Capturing Your Organization's Knowledge Assets").

Function 5: Using and Reusing Knowledge

Even if your organization establishes processes and systems for capturing, organizing, and sharing information, the information is not generating value if it is not used and reused. A salesperson in a knowledge-based company is often required to write up and submit a sales summary report on each sales opportunity to a common knowledge repository. The sales organization, in this case, benefits if it acquires a body of information that tells it how to win customers. The idea of learning from others' mistakes and failures helps the sales organization repeat the winning behaviors and reduce losses.

See Also   Chapter 5 presents an in-depth discussion on the processes of building and sustaining healthy collaborative environments.

Are You Ready for Implementation?

Now that you have assessed the potential value that a KM solution can create for your organization and seen the framework, you need to evaluate whether your organization is ready for such a change. You do that partly by weighing the value that the KM solution brings against its risks. Only then will you have a balanced view that you can use to judge a KM investment for your organization. In this section we look briefly at the costs incurred in establishing a KM solution. We then examine how understanding risk can help you target a KM solution to deliver the most business value. We look at the downside of risk— how it can jeopardize the initiative's success. Finally, we look at how a disciplined approach to risk management enables the team to determine how much to spend on managing the risks, establishing the program, and promoting its adoption.

The Risks of a KM Program

A team that is considering starting a KM effort should take into consideration the potential areas of risk. We have identified nine main areas that might jeopardize the success of your KM solution:

1. Cost of the solution

2. Organizational competencies

3. Proving success

4. KM adoption

5. Executive sponsorship

6. KM tools

7. Culture change

8. Inflexibility

9. Solution delivery process

The team needs to decide how much effort (and cost) it should commit to mitigating these risks. Contemporary businesses regularly assess corporate investments for risks. Risks are inherent in any activity that has an element of uncertainty, so the key to business success is not to make every possible attempt to avoid risks, but rather to identify and manage risks. Managing risks includes identifying the risk (stating the risk clearly), qualifying (analyzing the probability that the risk will occur), responding (if the risk does occur, how will it be handled?) and documenting lessons learned at the end of the project to capture the knowledge.[1]

KM is more prone to risks than many other initiatives that compete for management attention. That is because it is a relatively new discipline and does not have a long track record. For the KM practitioner, risk is twofold:

- On one hand, much of the justification for KM emanates from risks—the risk you run when you do not have a KM solution in place. Managers fear that tacit knowledge will be unavailable when most needed, locked up in a cranium on a different continent, or, worse still, given early retirement during a periodic wave of downsizing. They know that much explicit knowledge is inaccessible at the point of need, hidden in manuals gathering dust on an office shelf. They see their organization repeating costly mistakes because they don't have the culture, processes, or tools to learn lessons from prior experience. All of these possibilities are areas where KM can improve effectiveness and create value.

- On the other hand, the implementation of a KM solution is itself inherently risky. Although you might be able to point to examples in the past where better information would have delivered value, it is unusual to be able to predict reliably where such value will be generated in the future.

Let's explore risks by detailing each of the nine major areas of risk.

The Cost of the Solution

In many ways the cost of implementing a KM solution is similar to that of implementing other information technology (IT) applications. A new solution places considerable risk and financial strain on your organization. You can break down costs into two parts:

- the upfront investment
- the subsequent operating costs of the solution

---

1. Harold Kerzner. *Project Management: A Systems Approach to Planning, Scheduling, and Controlling.* 7th ed. (New York: John Wiley & Sons, 2000).

Direct upfront costs typically include hardware for servers and client machine upgrades (if necessary), software licenses, people costs for development and testing, and the costs of any consulting advice and training. Indirect upfront costs include costs for management and other overhead, including time taken away from other activities for training. Operating costs include technical costs, such as maintaining the hardware and software, operating the system, and using networks and other underlying infrastructure. Managing the nontechnical aspects of the solution also has costs, such as the costs of any dedicated knowledge specialists—for example, the cost of a full-time employee leading, administering, and monitoring tasks needed to maintain and lead the KM environment. All of these costs should be part of your organization's normal project costing processes.

However, KM solutions are also likely to incur a number of other costs that might be hidden. Specifically, KM solutions require changes in behavior, so you and your KM team should plan and budget for activities and communication to make these changes. As with any change in work patterns, users may go through a transitional period when their performance degrades as they learn new ways of working. Remember to allow for this effect before the benefits start to accrue.

Organizational Competencies

Organizations need to balance their KM programs across three competencies:

- customer satisfaction
- product leadership
- organizational operations

Outstanding performance in one dimension might lead to prosperity, but falling short in another dimension might threaten the organization's survival. The challenge is that advances in one competency tend to bring down performance in others. So organizations have to decide how to prioritize these competencies.

You can use a KM program to help aim a KM initiative at the areas where lack of accessible knowledge poses the greatest threat. By aligning the goals of a KM initiative with the organization's business objectives, executives can use KM to reduce those risks that most threaten their fundamental strategy.

For example, if an engineering company is focused on customer intimacy, its strategy will be at risk if its KM system in that area is not world-class. The quality of the relationship with its key customers will be damaged if a new salesperson has to rediscover all the nuances of the customer's business that her predecessor had acquired or if it takes longer than necessary to resolve a technical issue because the customer's normal support engineer is on vacation. On the other hand, the company's needs for knowledge about product leadership and operational excellence may well be less demanding because these are less critical to its prosperity. A less mature approach to KM in these areas may suffice without creating undue risk, provided overall quality does not fall to a level that threatens the organization's survival.

Proving Success

Measuring a KM initiative's effectiveness can be one of the key challenges for a KM team. In Chapter 2, "Placing a Value on Your Knowledge Management Investment," we discussed the concepts of KM metrics—what should be measured and why. Without a credible measure of success, any initiative is at risk of losing sponsorship and support and, as we will see later, sponsorship and support are particularly critical to a KM initiative's success. In Chapter 5 you will find a detailed discussion on the types of measures appropriate to various KM objectives. In theory, it should be possible to develop metrics that provide the in-process measures to support the value chain used to quantify the justification for the initiative.

See Also   Chapter 9, "Measuring the Effectiveness of Your Repository," for information about KM measurement technology enablement.

However, in practice this measurement faces two difficulties:

- **Measures of activity rarely measure impact.**   For instance, it is easy to measure how many documents are submitted to a repository and how often they are downloaded; it is much harder to place a value on a document in the repository or to confirm that a document has been read, let alone used, after it is downloaded.

- **Measures of impact rarely prove causality.** For instance, suppose a technical customer support department introduces a KM system to allow customers direct access to its technical knowledge base. Such a system could be justified by the reduced demand from customers for advice from support engineers. Eighteen months later, they may indeed find that they have reduced their support headcount, but this may be due to better product quality or customer training programs—or even simply to a tougher recruitment market. The KM application is just one factor contributing to the change.

This risk will not go away. To avoid this risk, you need to align the objectives of the KM program with business success criteria, to develop a set of evaluations that reflect this alignment, and to support these with regular surveys of key stakeholders to validate the qualitative aspects.

KM Adoption

Probably the best-publicized risk associated with KM systems is that the level of adoption fails to meet expectations. KM solutions involve two groups of users—knowledge creators and knowledge users. For most applications, participation by one or both of these groups is only voluntary—that is, they can continue to perform their role without using the KM application. KM practitioners must, therefore, pay special attention to motivating both groups of users.

Knowledge creators may view KM as a threat to their prestige, or perhaps even their livelihood. After all, if you are the only person who truly understands how to solve a particular technical issue, why should you be interested in sharing this knowledge? It dilutes your expertise, reduces your worth to the organization, and may mean that it can survive using less skilled (and hence less expensive) personnel.

Knowledge users may also lack enthusiasm. They may perceive their role as being "dumbed down." For instance, the hardware engineer no longer has to understand how each component works but merely has to look up an error condition in the "system" and replace the board as indicated.

To address this risk, an effective communications and recognition program must support any KM initiative. The truly innovative problem-solvers must appreciate that not only does their worth to the organization increase the more they share their knowledge of existing problems and move on to solve new issues, but, equally important, their managers understand their value. Likewise, the knowledge user can be given new challenges that don't rely on repeating known solutions to problems. The hardware engineer needs to be converted to an attitude in which it is more important to resolve the customer's real problem—that their business is being disrupted—than to find the neatest technical solution. In either case, recognition and reward programs play an essential role in ensuring that the organization reinforces the new patterns of behavior that it is seeking to introduce.

Executive Sponsorship

Executive sponsorship for a new KM project is critical if the program is to be a success. The role of a KM sponsor (representative to upper management) involves much more than authorizing the expenditure for the initiative. Effective KM sponsors have special qualities of leadership and are called upon to give presentations in their area of expertise to the KM community at KM functions and gatherings.

- **The sponsor is the most appropriate executive.**   For users to adopt new behaviors, the sponsor needs to be in a position to influence reward and recognition systems across the entire community. This means that the sponsor should be in the direct line of management above all users.

- **The sponsor commits adequate resources for the initiative to succeed.**   Besides providing sufficient funding, the sponsor will need to commit significant time from all stakeholder groups and to allocate a quality team to work on the initiative.

- **The sponsorship is visible to all stakeholders.**   Without visibility, motivation will not affect all users.

- **The sponsorship is maintained throughout the initiative's lifetime.**   Sponsorship will be needed most when the initiative hits problems. The quantity or quality of knowledge contribution might dry up as contributors come under pressure to meet different business goals, or knowledge reuse rates might start to fall as knowledge users revert to old behavior patterns after the initial campaign to introduce the system.

Special challenges arise if the KM sponsor leaves the organization or moves to a new position. It is critical that the replacement maintain commitment to the sponsorship role. The quality of the original business justification can be a deciding factor. If the KM initiative was founded on a clear business case that was aligned with the key business goals, the new sponsor can rapidly appreciate the initiative's value. If the organization has followed the KM Value Assessment model presented in Chapter 2, this should not be difficult. The more you can support the KM initiative with evidence of adoption and success, the easier the transition will be, so make every effort to measure the results of the initiative and their impact.

KM Tools

The earlier discussion on the risk of low user adoption focused on the motivation of users to change their behavior. As in any case in which change has to be managed, users need a compelling reason to work differently—and they also need to see that the change is easy to accomplish. Techniques for creating usable solutions have been well publicized elsewhere, even if they remain underutilized. They rely primarily on working with real users to understand how they work and figure out how these work patterns can be improved by introducing a new process. Unfortunately, too many solutions simply add more work for the user.

KM systems typically make life easier either for the contributor or for the knowledge reuser, but not both. The reason for this involves the responsibility for indexing and metadata. The contributor would prefer to simply submit material into the system without codifying metadata, entering keywords, and so on. On the other hand, knowledge users need to be able to find the most appropriate information as rapidly as possible, so they want to enter the minimum amount of information necessary to retrieve the most appropriate information. The solution to this problem may put more work on the contributor or on the knowledge user. Or it may introduce a third party to codify the knowledge or use automated tools to help. More likely, the solution will use a combination of these approaches. To be effective, it must be based on the underlying principles of designing for usability and it must take into account the full knowledge life cycle.

Culture Change

When you introduce a systems-based approach, the group dynamics that made a community-based approach viable may be destroyed. Organizations fail when they adopt a KM strategy that straddles both a document-centric strategy and a collaboration strategy.

In introducing its own KM initiative in 1999, Microsoft Consulting Services (MCS) faced a dilemma. Over the years it had developed a strong culture of mutual help: consultants provided informal assistance to one another in resolving problems through informal means such as discussion forums and e-mail aliases. These methods were reinforced by occasional face-to-face meetings at technical conferences. However, and perhaps as a consequence, previous attempts to formalize the capture of knowledge had failed to sustain momentum. The designers of a new MCS KM initiative were acutely aware that introducing a formal system might risk damaging the informal processes and the culture of cooperation, which had served the group well in the past. So they deliberately created a knowledge repository designed around communities of interest. They reinforced the existing culture by providing better-focused discussion groups and e-mail aliases, but they added Webcasts, online conferences, and virtual meetings. Moreover, the community members elected the subject matter experts (SMEs), giving them formal recognition; the experts were given the responsibility for reviewing documents submitted to the repository. Over 9000 knowledge assets (KAs) were collected by 2001. But SMEs approved only 10 percent of the KAs as validated repeatable quality knowledge; the reasons involved a combination of factors, including lack of SME time, lack of commitment to the process, and lack of needs assessment (see Chapter 7 for information on needs and gap analysis). The reward and recognition program put in place favored the *collection* of documents and other explicit assets (like code samples and diagrams). The program is now being revised to focus attention on, reward, and recognize using stored knowledge, finding and exchanging expertise, and ensuring content quality. The focus of the program, what is rewarded and what is measured, is by and large what the program will deliver.

Inflexibility

Although a disciplined approach to understanding the goals and performance metrics of a KM initiative can reduce the uncertainty of creating value, KM remains inherently unpredictable. In addition to the uncertainties of the business environment and the capabilities of the technology itself, which affect all IT applications, KM depends on a change in working behavior. As a result, few KM initiatives are likely to follow their original plans exactly. In some cases the changes may be subtle, such as refinement of the metadata used to organize a knowledge repository; in other cases more profound changes may be required, affecting the application's fundamental design and how it is implemented.

Retaining the flexibility to make these alterations places two types of demand on KM practitioners:

- They need to retain technical flexibility by designing their solution with this flexibility as a specific goal wherever feasible. Although buying KM software from a vendor may prove attractive at the outset and may accelerate the initial technical implementation, it may also lock the organization into an inappropriate approach and may not allow the solution to be customized for unique working patterns. For example, if the software you purchased lacks the capability to develop online reports, you may not be able to measure the communities' participation levels. A component-based architecture, as described in Part III, "The Technology of Knowledge Management," often provides a better approach, allowing the solution to evolve as the organization learns throughout the experience of implementation.

- The team itself needs to maintain a high degree of organizational agility. It should regularly review its progress and look critically at the performance metrics to validate whether the original plans are being achieved. It should also look for further opportunities for growth. For example, if the current system points out the number of times a KA has been used, the next step in the system's evolution might be to rate the quality of often reused KA.

Solution Delivery Process

A final implementation risk involves the methods used to deliver the IT solution. In the previous sections we identified a number of criteria that may be critical for the success of an initiative: providing a solution that is genuinely usable, retaining agility to adapt the solution based on feedback and reviews, and ensuring rapid delivery. In many organizations the in-house development team is constrained by its own objectives to adopt a less user-centered approach. Likewise, many external vendors have adopted methodologies that do not focus on these as criteria for success.

Implementation teams should therefore look closely at the methods that their technology solution uses, whether in-house or external, to see how well they support the specific needs of this type of work. The Microsoft Solutions Framework (a software development process created and used by Microsoft Consulting Services) includes three core principles that address these criteria and that might be useful to keep in mind:

- The end user's need for a usable solution is a critical contribution to the design process; one of the core roles within the development group is to represent the user experience.

- The principle of "baseline early, freeze late" applies a change management discipline to all deliverables, including designs and plans, allowing changes to be incorporated throughout the development life cycle.

- The concept of versioned releases proposes a regime of rapid, incremental releases, ensuring that users get early experience and can provide early feedback.

Managing Risks

Considering such a wide range of risks, a disciplined approach to risk management becomes essential. But how much should you spend on managing these uncertainties? Overspending reduces the value created by the initiative, but underspending may threaten your ability to achieve the project's goals.

Here are a few principles of risk management:

- Create a no-blame culture where risks can be identified without fear of repercussions.

- State each risk clearly and assess its probability and impact on success.

- Devise a strategy for each risk; focus on managing the highest-impact risks first. For the higher-impact risks, develop a mitigation strategy and include it in the project plans and costing. Low-impact risks can be left unmanaged if the costs outweigh the exposure.

- Monitor the mitigation strategy's effectiveness.

- Review the status of risks regularly and revise the strategies for risks if you change your view of their impact.

Summary

Regardless of your organization's size, your solution for content collection and reuse in a KM environment requires implementing five key functions:

- a way to support creating knowledge

- a way to support capturing knowledge

- a means of organizing content

- a method of sharing and distributing knowledge

- a means to support use and reuse of content

Make sure that you are ready to implement your KM solution by developing a comprehensive risk program. As a team, make sure to evaluate and plan for risks before beginning the implementation.

Once you identify the risks that your organization faces, make a plan to manage them. State risks clearly, analyze the probability that the risk will occur, and, if the risk is present in your environment, indicate how it will be handled.

Focus attention on creating a solid foundation (the methods and means) for distributing and reusing business critical knowledge. As important as content production, distribution, and consumption are, remember that one of the true values of KM in a knowledge-based economy is its ability to foster creativity and innovation.

Building involves risk

Manage risk for success

Creating and Sustaining Communities of Practice

There are plenty of teams in every sport that have great players and never win titles. Most of the time, those players aren't willing to sacrifice for the greater good of the team. The funny thing is, in the end, their unwillingness to sacrifice only makes individual goals more difficult to achieve. One thing I believe to the fullest is that if you think and achieve as a team, the individual accolades will take care of themselves. Talent wins games, but teamwork and intelligence win championships.

Michael Jordan, professional basketball player

As we discussed in the last chapter, knowledge management (KM) environments require three components:

- a virtual space (communities in which people can share and create)
- a technology foundation (the library function)
- processes to glue these elements together

This chapter addresses the first of these components: virtual communities.

Knowledge sharing does not come naturally to anyone, especially in highly competitive company environments. For this reason, **communities of practice (CoPs)** are an excellent way to encourage peer-level participation in the KM space. In this chapter we will discuss the benefits of CoPs, how to structure them to align with the business objectives as well as the participants' goals, and, finally, how to sustain communities of practice.

The Benefit of Communities

Communities of practice are fast becoming recognized as one of the most effective ways to link people who need knowledge with the sources of knowledge (both explicit and tacit). These groups help organizations maintain an edge in the marketplace by giving employees a convenient way to share knowledge electronically in virtual space—across time zones, continents, cultures, and other barriers. In the geographically dispersed knowledge era, technology-enabled CoPs have taken the place of the more informal hallway or lunchroom gatherings.

A critical challenge for knowledge workers is getting hold of organized information. It is often difficult for employees to add knowledge contribution or knowledge sharing to their list of work tasks. But when you create peer groups with common interests, employees are more likely to contribute knowledge assets. Members see the immediate gain they derive from getting information from others in the group. CoPs tap into creativity at work and promote the adoption of KM behavior at every layer of an organization by combining working, learning, and innovating in virtual groups. They form the dynamic social infrastructure required for knowledge sharing.

At its simplest level, a CoP is a group of people who work together formally and informally over a period of time. Its members might perform the same or a similar job, collaborate on shared tasks, or share an interest in a subject area. A CoP is cohesive because its members have a common sense of purpose and a need to collaborate. A CoP does not have to be an internal work group. External CoPs, such as the Microsoft Network (MSN) Visual Basic users group, successfully support developers around the world. Global enterprises clearly benefit from the ability to provide peer groups to geographically dispersed knowledge workers, rendering physical location no longer a barrier to the peer relationship.

Communities of practice can be either managed (such as the Microsoft Consulting Services Database/Data Warehousing Community for internal Microsoft consultants) or unmanaged (such as the MSN Developers Community, which is a public community open to all developers regardless of company affiliation). CoPs represent efforts by companies, organizations, or collective groups to organize people around subject areas. Internet providers, such as MSN, and company intranets can provide virtual electronic space in which unmanaged communities can share their knowledge. Basically, in unmanaged communities knowledge is shared by people who may or may not have any other relationship. Unmanaged communities in this sense are like the free market, with an open exchange of services and information that may or may not lead to lasting personal or professional relationships. Internal managed CoPs, on the other hand, provide not only the benefit of collaboration but also an opportunity to build internal relationships and company networks regardless of physical location. An enterprise can focus the benefit of collaborative KM through managed CoPs. The same concepts can be applied to managed CoPs and informal Internet or other unmanaged communities.

The Structure of Communities

Before you establish a structure for all the potential CoPs in your organization, it is important to decide what each community will focus on and what its relationship to the strategic business objectives will be. When you tie communities to business strategy, the community members can focus and support the broader organizational objectives. The focus, and even the primary direction, of a managed community should be responsive to the strategic business directives within a company. As a leader and member of the Microsoft Consulting Services (MCS) Commerce community (an internal managed CoP that focuses on Microsoft Commerce Server), this author has experienced the demands of shifting business goals on CoPs. It was clear that once Microsoft's business objectives moved to selling more end-to-end solutions, we needed to change the focus of our Commerce community away from a strictly technology focus (such as Commerce Server implementation) to a complete solution view (such as Microsoft Solutions Internet Business). As the business changed, the community leadership needed to guide a change in the community to keep it in line with the business strategy. The repository was examined and missing content was identified. We collected white papers, code samples, templates, and guides and organized them into chunks of information that covered the following categories: planning, developing, deploying, and operating the solution (see Chapter 7, "Capturing Your Organization's Knowledge Assets," for more information on how to structuring a knowledge index). The team advertised mini-training sessions (conference calls) and summits that supported the solution, while identifying who among us was a solutions expert. The experts conducted the conference calls and answered questions from the community. The community not only changed direction but also rallied together to support its members in making the transition. When CoPs and business objectives are aligned, KM gathers executive support and credibility.

CoPs are unique environments within which the business provides a judgment-free zone where employees can give, ask for, or exchange information. Community participants can pull needed information from peers or experts, and, when necessary, the business can push out subject-related information to a specific audience. This two-way push-pull knowledge exchange is a foundation of community purpose within a company.

You can categorize communities according to the business strategy that they address. Typical community structures might be based on subject areas (such as products) or industry segments (such as finance or customer relationship management [CRM]).

- **Product or technology communities**   generally focus on the business's specific product/technology base. Participants are generally in these communities because of interest rather than job assignment.

- **Role or function communities**   generally form around the current set of roles, such as project managers, trainers, and so on, within a company. Participants tend to move in and out of these communities based on their job assignments.

- **Industry or market segment communities**   are generally formed around the company's current interest in the marketplace, and the members concentrate on supporting or selling these unique markets for the company.

- **Special Interest Groups (SIGs)**   are subgroups that often form within communities to explore very specialized areas of interest. Joining a SIG does not require the member to change communities, but it does allow the member to explore a subject area with other interested parties within the community.

Product or Technology Communities

A common form of CoP is a group that focuses on a specific product or technology. Product or technology communities in a manufacturing business might be materials management or structural engineering groups. In a technology company such as Microsoft, you might have a database or operating systems community. The member's level or role does not matter. In any given community you might have members who range from assistants to general managers. The requirement for membership is a common interest in the subject.

In a product or technology community, as demonstrated in Figure 5-1, content is requested from the knowledge worker into the community and supplied to the community by specialists, such as warehouse expeditors or health-safety educators, or in the case of technology, information technology (IT) specialists or senior consultants.

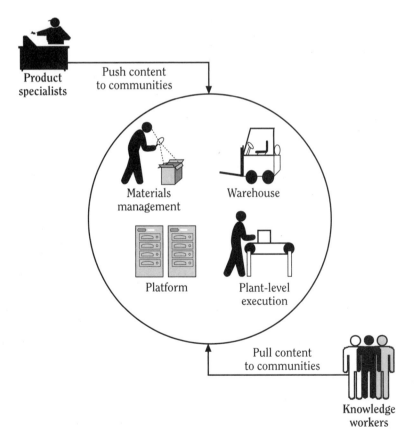

Figure 5-1. *Product or Technology Communities*

Role or Function Communities

In role or function communities, as demonstrated Figure 5-2, members work in a certain position, such as sales manager or administrative assistant, or in a certain area, such as production or sales. An example of a function-based community for a global business is a regional community, such as Asia, Europe, or the Americas. An example of a role-based community is project management or sales.

These communities supply templates and practices to the knowledge worker and receive, as knowledge assets (KAs), case studies from work assignments and experience from the knowledge worker.

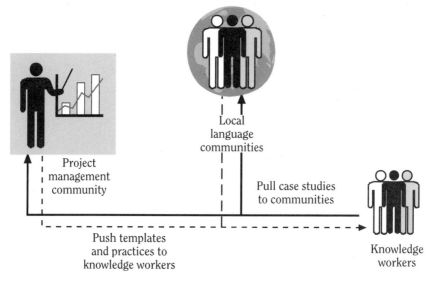

Figure 5-2. *Role or Function Communities*

Industry-Focused or Market-Focused Communities

Members of industry-focused or market-focused communities, as demonstrated in Figure 5-3, have jobs across product sectors and roles in the organization. Financial services, supply chain, and telecommunications are examples of industry or market communities. People tend to come in and out of these communities based on their current assignment or interests. For example, a specialist in technology platform installation for Microsoft may at one point concentrate on the financial and banking marketplace and at another point on the retail marketplace. This platform specialist may continue to be a member of the platforms (technology-based) community but would leave the financial-banking community upon being reassigned to the retail sector.

The information flow supplies business and industry information to the knowledge workers. In turn, the knowledge worker requests content back as KAs to the industry or market-focused communities after completing a customer project or workshop.

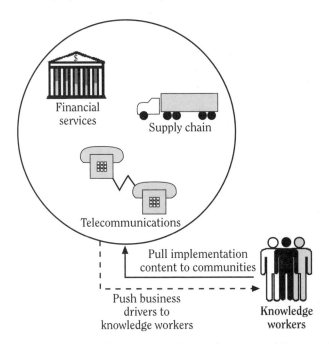

Figure 5-3. *Industry-Focused or Market-Focused Communities*

Special Interest Groups Within Communities (Subtypes)

Often, areas of interest do not easily fit into one community. SIGs are a way to manage a wide range of interest areas that spring up within one community but may have applications in other communities. An example of a SIG in a high-technology company might be security. In Table 5-1, note that security spans several technical and business communities (such as database and financial services), but it has a specific focus of interest to all its members. A SIG has its home in one community, but it allows members of other communities to participate. This makes it possible for many communities to address varied interests and business strategies without requiring people to join more communities. It also reduces redundancy of information and effort. The following table demonstrates the intersection between sample communities and SIGs.

Table 5-1.   Special Interest Groups

Examples of Communities	Deployment	Management	Mobility	Operations	Security
Data Warehouse (interest based)		P			P
Distributed Applications (interest based)	P				P
Financial Services (interest based)				P	P
Messaging (interest based)	P		H		P
Platforms (interest based)	H	P	P	H	H
Service Delivery (role based)		H			

H = SIG Home Community

P = Participatory Community

Starting a Community

Communities cannot exist without a common purpose, a means of communication, and basic organization. You can think of a community as a set of interconnected elements that come together to help the knowledge worker collaborate with others. What is important is that people are able to use community tools to get things done with other people. Three elements, as presented in Figure 5-4, make up most communities: supporting tools and processes (such as Web pages or methods for managing community content), collaborative structures (such as SIGs or conference calls), and people (such as a leader).

With the guidance of proactive leadership that motivates members to help one another, technology can enable community participants to contribute in useful ways. The leader can motivate knowledge workers to make useful contributions to the community so that they improve their reputation, get greater exposure in the company, and receive peer recognition. To make sure that the community is aligned with the business objective, an internally managed community should develop a community profile, or charter. The profile is not only a statement of the community's focus but also a declarative statement about how to perpetuate the membership and structure the community.

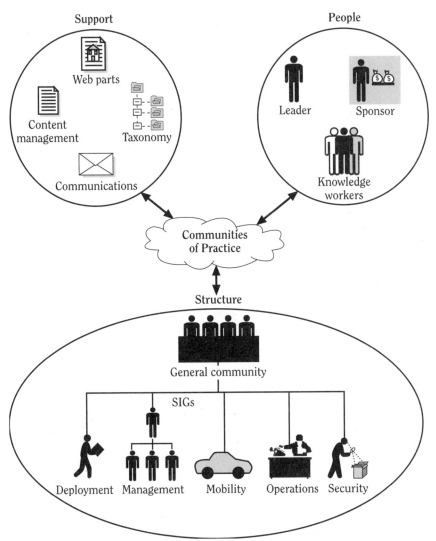

Figure 5-4. *Components of Communities of Practice*

Once the community focus is clearly understood and aligned with the business objectives, you can take steps to organize the community. These steps should include establishing:

- leadership and sponsorship
- a community profile
- a communication plan
- membership

Establishing a Leader

In a managed community the community leader (CL) is the organizer and catalyst who develops and sustains a healthy community. This individual may be a facilitator or subject matter expert (SME), but his or her most important quality is being a respected member of the peer group.

Establishing an Executive Sponsor

Your next step is to seek an executive sponsor. The executive sponsor is the single most important factor in recruiting members and obtaining funding. Without executive sponsorship and encouragement from management, members will lose their enthusiasm and interest when they see that upper management does not value community efforts. An executive sponsor not only recognizes achievements, but also advocates KM behaviors to his or her peers and the larger organization.

Establishing a Community Profile

One of your early steps in starting a community should be to define its charter by writing a community profile. This document describes the community and establishes its aims and operating scope. The CL draws up the community's profile with the guidance of the community members, and if the organization has a centralized KM management group, the KM manager approves the profile. (If KM is centralized, the KM manager is responsible for ensuring consistency and providing direction across the communities as a whole.)

The community profile document should include a vision/scope statement, a mission statement, measurable objectives, and roles and responsibilities for the community, along with any other information needed to describe the community and how it operates. It should be formally reviewed once a year (but kept up to date at all times)—quarterly updates are recommended.

The following table shows the major sections of a profile.

Table 5-2. Sections of a Community Profile Document

Community Profile Section	Purpose
Vision/scope statement	Explains how the community intends to enable KM at a global level
Mission statement	States the value of the community and the benefits it will provide for its members
Roles and responsibilities	Lists generic community roles that should be identified with specific assignments; should be updated regularly.
Objectives	Lists measurable goals for community members, and improving business efficiency and quality

Vision/Scope and Mission Statements

The first step in creating the community profile is to determine the community's focus and to keep it in line with the organization's goals. With the focus in mind, the CL, executive sponsor, and key members can develop initial vision/scope and mission statements as well as establish community objectives. Defining critical success factors will help the leaders guide the community. As part of the community profile, the leader will need to describe community roles and responsibilities, as shown in Table 5-3, along with a description of the goals and objectives for each role, as shown in Table 5-4. The following are examples of a vision/scope statement and a mission statement from the MCS Commerce community:

Vision/scope statement.   The purpose of the Commerce community is to: facilitate the exchange, sharing, and reuse of Commerce-related issues, enterprise architecture, and collaborative solutions.

Mission statement.   The mission of the Commerce community is to enable field individuals to:

- Capture, submit, and share enterprise design and development experiences in the context of specific field experiences as challenged by a customer's environmental and business problems.
- Identify key technology leaders (experts) in the community.
- Provide a structured environment (both collaboratively and electronically) conducive to submitting and reusing.

- Identify guidelines or templates, or both, that can efficiently capture commerce designs and collaborative application development experiences.

- Promote the consumption of guidelines and templates in engagement work.

- Cultivate this structured knowledge through a Web site and through collaborative events.

- Increase the quality of solutions and services and reduce risk through identification and reuse of proven, reusable assets.

- Increase efficiency and reduce costs by leveraging KAs that are easily located and most relevant to provide the greatest reusability potential.

- Increase information flow and facilitate feedback loops between the product group and the field.

- Share competitive field intelligence.

Roles and Responsibilities

The following table provides a sample of the roles, responsibilities, and time allocation for community participants in a centralized and formally managed KM environment that the CL can use when discussing participation with prospective members. Distributed (regional or local KM operations), informal, and public KM environments may have different requirements or roles.

Table 5-3.   Roles and Responsibilities in the Profile

Role	Responsibilities	Time Commitment
Executive sponsor	Provides the community with upper-level management support and representation. Present at community events and announces rewards and recognitions. Level of commitment is defined in the initial request for sponsorship made by the community.	Time commitment varies and is outlined in the initial request for sponsorship made by the executive.
Community leader (CL)	Responsible for developing, launching, and managing the community. Sustains community growth and maintains collaboration, content, resources, and relationships. Ensures KAs are maintained and promotes knowledge submission and content sharing.	Full-time position.

Table 5-3.   Roles and Responsibilities in the Profile   *(continued)*

Role	Responsibilities	Time Commitment
Subject matter expert (SME)	A person elected by community members to keep the community running cohesively. Mentors and assists in driving issues through the community. Important to have broad mix of skills, interests, roles, and locations.	One to three days per month or full time.
Special Interest Group (SIG) leader (SL)	Responsible for developing, launching, and managing a SIG, working closely with the CL. Typically filled by one of the SMEs. Needs to be an acknowledged expert in the area addressed by the SIG.	Approximately two to four days per month, depending on the activity within the group.
Expert	Community member identified by CL as a person who is a key knowledge holder but does not have a leadership position. CL may use the following criteria to identify an expert: business value and volume of the expert's downloaded submissions, frequency of response to community distribution lists (DLs), surveys of community members to vote for the experts.	No formal allocation.
Community member	Requests membership based on interest, role/function, or business focus. Participates in community activities; contributes and reuses KAs, and collaborates with other communities' members when appropriate.	No formal allocation.
Guest	No formal role in community but wants to observe before taking part in it.	No formal allocation.
Launch Team (LT) (optional)	One option to the early development of KAs might be a prelaunch subset of members who seed the repository with reusable content prior to launch. Size of team depends on resources available, quantity of existing local content, and time available prior to community launch.	Time allocation can vary depending on the number of team members and the amount of existing content to be migrated to the repository.

Depending on the requirements of your organization, you might want to add roles for content managers and local KM managers to this list. For additional information on content management, including validation and editing, see Chapter 7.

Objectives

The community profile needs to describe performance plans for its community. The performance plan goals and objectives describe how community members should build KM into their daily work. The goals and objectives should focus on major KM work behaviors, such as knowledge development, knowledge reuse, and knowledge sharing. Community members with the most seniority or subject matter experience, or both, should have goals and objectives that aim for the highest contribution targets. If the member is less senior or in need of experience, the goals and objectives should aim at reuse targets. Table 5-4 outlines a few examples of community goals and objectives:

Table 5-4.   Goals and Objectives

Goal/Objective	Description
View	Regularly log on to the community Web page.
Join	Join one community of practice.
Communicate	Regularly exchange tacit knowledge at community conference calls.
Reuse	Regularly use explicit content items for education and on company business.
Develop	Submit two documents to the repository per year.
Event	Attend two events per year.
Present	Deliver information at one event per year.
Mentor	Mentor team members, guiding knowledge reuse and submissions around business topics.
Review	Evaluate and review content to ensure that high-quality content is submitted to the repository.

Connecting Objectives to Roles in the Profile

Once you outline the basic objectives, you should map the objectives to the community participants, as shown in Table 5-5. It will be easy to see from this mapping process what the community performance goals for the different roles in the community are.

Table 5-5.   Mapping Participants and Objectives

Participants	Objectives								
	View	Join	Communicate	Event	Reuse	Present	Develop	Mentor	Review
Subject matter expert	X	X	X	X	X	X	X	X	X
Special interest group leader	X	X	X	X	X	X	X	X	X
Expert	X	X	X	X	X		X		
Community member	X	X	X	X	X		X		
Community leader	X	X	X	X		X			
Community executive sponsor	X	X				X			
Migration team	X	X			X				
Guest	X								

The community should post its current profile on its Web site so that community members can see what the community goals are and act (and comment) on them appropriately. Once you have developed your profile, you are ready to move forward and launch your community.

Establishing Communications Through a Community Web Page

In the electronic age the Web is the primary way to bring people, content, and collaboration together. Think of the Web site as the community's home. If the members need information, they go home to find it. They can seek content that already resides in the repository or talk with peers or experts in the chat room. The community Web page provides an environment in which members can access communication, collaborative events, member profiles, and training materials. It is also where members can search the global repository of community documents. Good content, fresh news, and connectivity will keep members passionate about the community site.

One option for the Web page is to use Microsoft SharePoint Portal Server, which provides an easy way to create corporate Web portals and integrate document management and search capabilities. Web portals gather information from many different sources in one convenient place. SharePoint Portal Server creates a Web portal known as the dashboard site that is automatically created during installation. The dashboard offers a centralized access point for finding and managing information. A digital dashboard consists of reusable, customizable Web parts (locations on a Web page) that can present information from a wide variety of sources. These are typically separate pages within the site that are accessible through links from the main page.

Table 5-6.   Possible Components of a Community Web Site

Web Part	Description
Community Table of Contents	Lists all the parts of the Web site that members can reach. Editable by the CL. Supports the community's focus.
Learning Access	Links user to community-related training sites.
Events Information	Information about events, training opportunities, or other activities of interest.
Current Topics	Articles and links to external Web sites that pertain to the community's focus and interests. These have expiration dates and move to Warm Topics section when they expire.
Warm Topics	Automatically populated when Current Topics expire. Typically moved to an archive section after three months, but can vary as needed.
Repository News	Highlights the most recent submissions made by community members.
Activity Counter	Displays number of sites visited by the individual, total site visits, distinct visitors, total downloads, and distinct downloaders. Also displays person with most submissions, person with most downloads, and names of authors of 10 most frequently downloaded documents.
Instant Messenger	Enables community members to collaborate by sending instant messages to one another and to submit and receive questions and answers instantaneously.
Metrics	Displays total submissions, total members, and the individual's total submissions.
My Links	Lets a member create a link to his or her favorite sites. The links will then be displayed on the Web site.

See Also   Examples of these Web parts can be found in Chapter 9, "Measuring the Effectiveness of Your Repository" and Chapter 10, "Knowledge Searching and Services."

The community leader fills out the categories with community-specific information. It is up to the leader to ensure that the community Web page encourages collaboration. Remember to change the site frequently to keep people coming back. The Web site should be easy to use, and the steps a user has to take to join the community should be both visible and intuitive.

Establishing Membership

To attract and keep members, a community must be compelling. The community's core theme must engage the members by providing a way to develop, preserve, use, and share knowledge. To do this, a community's focus and discussions must be relevant to the community members. If the members are not interested in the subjects that are discussed, the community will not survive.

Recruiting members is vital for supporting and sustaining the scope outlined in your community vision and mission. Your community's scope can be broad, but all subjects must be important to your organization's maintenance and growth. The scope of managed communities should link to the larger organizational and individual goals and objectives. When the community's scope is aligned with business goals, its members will continue to see their participation as important and relevant.

Advertise

You will need to promote your new community by advertising its focus, goals, and benefits to the organization at large. You can advertise in a variety of ways: through newsletters, company meetings, and mass mailings to people in your company. One-on-one communication among workers and word of mouth from other interested members are both excellent ways to begin a new community with a core group of members. Community-sponsored events and conferences are also good advertising tools. They encourage industry and product experts to share knowledge with community members.

See Also   Now that your community is set up, you will need to start adding to its store of knowledge. See Chapter 7 for details on collecting knowledge within a community.

Sustaining Communities of Practice

Once you have laid the groundwork for your new CoP, the next challenge is to sustain it. Sustaining CoPs involves understanding how to keep the passion alive while encouraging evolution and reinvention over time. You can sustain passion by communicating, promoting, and rewarding the desired behaviors. In Chapter 2, "Placing a Value on Your Knowledge Management Investment," we discussed the theory of KM metrics, and in this section we will discuss how they support community participation.

Communicating Within Communities

Communication is the single most critical element in the success of a new community. If members are not fully informed of the community's events, opportunities for collaboration, and content, they cannot participate.

You can use a variety of methods to exchange ideas among members of a community. Choose the methods of communicating that best fit your company's culture and infrastructure. Try to test the results of using your communication method to make sure your target audience is hearing you. Table 5-7 lists community audiences and potential communication methods that have proven successful for those audiences.

Table 5-7. Communication Methods for Audience Types

Audience to Reach	Communication Method	When the Method Works Best
Community members	E-mail	For any communication that requires fast action of members.
Community members, SMEs, and SLs	Conference calls	For monthly working meetings among SMEs or SLs to conduct community business. In addition, for all community meetings to share knowledge from experts with the community at large.
Community members	Instant training	Technology such as Webcasts (live streaming media over the Web) or video teleconferencing (VTC) that allows dial-up to training events. Usually these events address specific topics and are brief.
SMEs, SLs, and community members	Summits/ conferences	These are periodic collaborative events that focus on high-interest topics.
Community leader	Process	For members to answer questions, surveys, and special requests from the CL. In most cases the feedback is received through e-mail; however, telephone and Webcasts are frequently used.
Community members	Web site	To share current events and topics.

Promoting Leadership in the Community

Some community members are experts in a specific subject area. It is therefore important to locate, promote, and reinforce this subject matter expertise (and SME status) within the community. SMEs not only serve as part of the community leadership but also can be elected to lead special interest groups within the community, validate community knowledge (in a repository), and educate others or simply be available to assist others. It is recommended that SME and SIG leader elections or appointments be held once a year (preferably coinciding with the fiscal year for budgeting purposes). The community members nominate candidates from the community and then the community votes on the nominees.

A community usually has more than one SME. The number a community needs depends on:

- The number of submissions to be reviewed and edited on a regular basis to support expected content flow

- The complexity and specificity of the community content

- The number of collaborative events and mentoring activities that are needed to support tasks that are not related to content

Microsoft Consulting Services has found that a virtual group of SMEs at the ratio of one to every 250 community members provides a good response time for content review and community activity support. This ratio was compiled from MCS's community of practice expertise over the past two years.

Having the right skills is a fundamental component of being a SME. All SMEs should meet the following criteria:

- Demonstrate communication and leadership skills within the existing community

- Have experience as a mentor in the areas relevant to the community

- Be identified as a "go-to" person for community information, specializing in key relevant knowledge areas

- Show expertise in key community technology areas (through project execution, training, or certification)

- Be capable of reviewing content specific to the community focus (white papers, training, materials, and so on)

- Show strong participation in answering questions in community-related e-mail discussion groups

- Demonstrate ability to be a major knowledge creator and contributor

Even if someone has all these SME skills, that person may not be known well enough in the community to be elected a SME. To increase visibility in the community, an expert can do the following:

- Participate in community decisions such as the SME election process or identification of needed community events and news items

- Volunteer for community tasks like serving on the community start-up team (if one exists), submitting event topic ideas, and leading collaborative events

- Participate in community events by launching the kickoff, biweekly conference calls, special topic calls, and other collaborative events

- Facilitate and host community events such as speaking at company conferences and initiating and leading conference calls or collaborative events

- Submit content to the community repository

- Gain recognition for submitting highly reusable content and for hosting events

- Promote KM behaviors with day-to-day contacts

Motivating people to make contributions is a big challenge for a community's leaders: how do you get people who are already working 10- to 12-hour days to spend "just a little more time" to write down something that might help someone else—someone they may not know or who may never thank them? There needs to be a constant motion between personal discovery and shared experiences. Community leaders and SIG leaders can encourage collaboration through e-mail, voice mail, conference calls, community Web sites, conferences, summits, "airlifts" (technical training summits), and other events that focus on networking and sharing new ideas, best practices, and lessons learned.

Community leaders should also take a role in supporting and sustaining CoPs, such as by:

- recognizing individual achievement

- building group identity

- establishing incentives and rewarding participation

- celebrating successes

- delivering value

It is imperative to build strong relationships among the executive sponsor, the CL, the SIG leader, SMEs, and community members. To maintain a barometer of how the CoP is doing, it is helpful to have a good set of measures (such as the number of participants at each event or the number of visits that members make to the Web page) that track the CoP's health and effectiveness. Beyond just developing a measurement system, organizations must establish an accountability structure that is coordinated with the support structure for the community.

Some key ways for leaders to help sustain CoPs include having an efficient community management structure; maintaining community pride and loyalty; having leaders who epitomize these qualities and are able to lead and manage wisely while remaining committed to the community's welfare; and providing a formal channel to address complaints, concerns, or advice. It is extremely important for CoPs to incorporate concern for participating and sustaining into all of the decision-making that is related to community development.

Successful recognition and reward programs provide incentives and the means to get members to participate in a community. As part of the agreement with the executive sponsor, the CL should make sure that throughout the organization, spending time participating in KM is one of the goals of every (appropriate) person in the organization. Communities that do not recognize and promote their members on a fair and equitable basis soon lose them.

Rewards and Recognition

Rewards and recognition encourage community members to develop, share, and reuse knowledge while building the KM community. As a foundation, members should include KM goals in their personal performance plan so that part of their job requirements include contributing to a community. The more active members become in the community, the more points they receive toward their community involvement objective at review time.

At the community level, a system of rewards and recognition brings outstanding KM achievement and community participation to the attention of peers, management, and executives. Members can receive rewards and recognition over two time periods: the prelaunch phase (if applicable) and throughout the year. You should ensure that the criteria for rewards and recognition are well known at the start of the evaluation period. Make sure that the criteria:

- are meaningful and valuable to community members
- are distributed fairly

- are presented in a timely manner
- can be shared with family and friends

Above all, community members want to be recognized for their contributions. To make sure that the community's rewards and recognition program is appropriate, meet with a subset of the community members (such as the SMEs and executive sponsors) to review and finalize the design of this plan. Also, when you design rewards and recognition programs, consider geographical constraints (a member in Singapore might not be able to come to a rewards dinner in New York) and the appropriateness of the rewards. And think creatively about how the community can award its members. You might consider building a point system-based "knowledge broker" program, as suggested by Professor Nick Bontis of McMasters University. A knowledge exchange program would allocate points for each KM behavior performed by participants according to the system's business rules and the organization's needs. For example, you award more points for KAs that fill high-priority content gaps than for the addition of redundant materials. You award points for the contribution and consumption of KAs, expertise, and tacit-to-tacit knowledge exchange (such as answering questions on an e-mail discussion).[1] Points can be exchanged for rewards, and they are a way for leaders to highlight top performers.

Measuring Success

As we described in Chapter 2, what gets measured gets managed. Effective KM often fundamentally changes how we do business: community members build KM goals into their performance plan, and management needs to incorporate KM into how business is conducted. KM participants contribute knowledge by capturing their experiences and submitting the reused KAs (for example, documentation, templates, or other assets in the repository that have been upgraded or used in unique ways). Goals and objectives, coupled with the proper time allocation, enable members to practice KM. Communities are outstanding vehicles for publishing the accomplishments of members who practice good KM behaviors as well as for rewarding groups and managers who promote and support KM as part of the work environment by recognizing their achievements. A program of organized and well-presented measurement is critical to a well-received recognition and reward program.

---

1. "Rewarding Knowledge," *KMWorld* 10, no. 9, (October 2001): 1.

You can generally program a KM system (that is, the technology that supports the KM activities) to collect the data you need to present information on community participation and activities. A good set of statistics and trends will help the community's leaders and managers guide the community in meeting the goals and objectives that it set up in its community profile. At first, communities may collect only simple measures (such as the number of documents submitted in a given month) and report only activity statistics (such as the number of visits to the Web site). These statistics can be tracked on a simple set of community vitality reports (as described below) with a simple summary statement that highlights positive trends and challenges. As the process matures, the community should adopt the KVA framework, as described in Chapter 2.

Individual member submission and reuse metrics will give you better insight into individual behavior. By treating community members as knowledge consumers and knowledge producers, you can gain greater insight at the level at which content is shared. Think of a knowledge transaction as a consumer product: connecting consumers (members who reuse knowledge) with producers (submitters of knowledge) will over time improve the process of knowledge product development (that is, content creation). Submitters can continuously improve their knowledge by understanding how others reuse it. As the community recognizes members who create the most reusable knowledge (content that is high quality and focused), others will emulate the behavior. Knowledge consumers who are rewarded for their behavior will not only repeat the behavior but also encourage others to follow in their footsteps.

What to Monitor

It is the CL's responsibility to clearly understand the activities and issues within the community to ensure an active and valuable membership. Some examples of activities to monitor are:

- Status of the submission queues (marked submissions waiting to be reviewed). Submissions should not be left in the queue for too long. They should be inserted into the repository (accepted), reviewed by a SME, and accepted or rejected.

- Sudden changes in the trends of submissions. Spikes or reductions in submissions may be explainable, but the CL should know the reason.

- Sudden spikes or reductions in visits to the community Web page.

- Changes in conference call participation.
- Significant changes in traffic on community e-mail discussion groups.
- Significant regional variations. If one team is more active than others, perhaps it has come across a problem that others could help with.
- SIGs that are showing any of the above symptoms.

One of the CL's tasks is to find out what could affect the community (for example, a product launch) and feed this information back to the community members.

Vitality Reports

Once you have some data about basic community activities (such as Web site visits) or KAs (such as the number of documents submitted by members), you can generate reports to summarize and describe the trends you have seen. **Vitality reports** are statistics and trends that allow the community to quickly see how healthy it is in terms of content submission and collaboration participation. Vitality reports summarize data about individual, business unit, and community activities by time period (usually by month). You can choose to track a variety of data in your vitality report. The following are some examples of vitality statistics.

Global Submissions

This number shows the submission rate and growth in content (inventory) in the repository each month. The data can be presented according to any criteria (such as community product) that clearly align the content to the business goals.

Distinct Contributors (Submitters)

This data reveals the breadth of contributors—how many community members are submitting content each month. In addition, this report measures whether a broad spectrum of community members is participating or if only a few people are contributing the bulk of the content.

Distinct Downloaders

This data shows how many community members are consuming content each month. This is another breadth measurement that helps to answer the question: do we have wide or narrow support from the community?

Distinct Site Views

This data measures how many community members visit the Web site each month. Community members may not always produce or consume, but by visiting the site, they are "active" in the community.

Net Change in Membership

This data monitors community membership change on a monthly basis. This figure is important during the early phases of a community's development, but it becomes less important as a community matures. As a community matures, it tends to reach a stable population. At this point you can watch just for sudden changes.

Web Site Reporting

Each community Web site might include counters to collect visitation data. We have found great value in continuously updating the online community health metrics. The following are indicators you might want to consider measuring:

- Total site visits
- Total downloads
- Most submissions (by author)
- Total submissions (in the repository)
- Total submissions (by community)
- Distinct visitors
- Distinct downloaders
- Authors most frequently downloaded
- Total members

As soon as the content repository is set up, use vitality reports to track the community's progress. Doing so will give you historical insight that will help you understand future community growth. Once you have started, generate vitality reports monthly, communicating the information through the community newsletter and the community Web page. Distribute the reports monthly to the management and quarterly to the executive sponsors.

Business Unit Scorecard

You can further refine a vitality report by viewing a **business unit scorecard,** which breaks down the vitality report data by group. Giving each business group its own report card can spur district and local groups to competition, thus building global communities while breaking down regional barriers. Submissions and participation are the metrics that might be included. The scorecard can communicate levels of accomplishment by utilizing a three-tiered system: red—*needs improvement,* yellow—*room for improvement,* and green—*currently successful.* The benchmarks will change as a community grows.

Vitality reports and business unit scorecards serve as a "community mirror," reflecting areas that are doing well and areas that need improvement: Who is submitting? Who is reusing? Who is participating? Who is innovating? Perhaps most importantly, who is not? Additionally, this data spurs healthy, intracommunity competition.

Summary

CoPs are vital links in an overall KM strategy. CoPs focus on the promotion and adoption of collaborative work behaviors as the foundation of value creation. To achieve this goal, the community's leaders must have the support and sponsorship of the business leaders, the respect of their peers in the community, and a passion for their mission. The community is the touch point for a virtual, and often geographically dispersed, group of people whose common bond is conceptual rather than physical. Although the knowledge worker's work environment is a far cry from the brick-and-mortar factory of an earlier generation, the same need for connectivity, common goals, and peer approval still exists. Good CoPs can serve as this common ground if the leadership tends to the community's need for connectivity, organization, and problem-solving.

Connect people with goals

Goals drive value

Building Taxonomies

As content grows in the electronic world, it is apparent that simply turning a search engine loose on a collection of information will not give the hoped for improvements in productivity and profits promised by e-business. Taxonomies are the missing link.

*Mike Crandall, former Knowledge Architect Manager,
Microsoft Corporation[1]*

One of the beautiful aspects of language (and of the human mind) is the limitless and varied ways that we are able to translate our knowledge and needs into direct and indirect "speech acts" and actions. Metaphors, idioms, and synonyms, for example, can bring variety and precision to our conversations and our writings. And human brains are wonderful tools for inferring and learning the meanings of new ways of communicating. But this very variety presents KM systems with one of their biggest challenges. If an author of an information artifact (such as a document or an answer in an e-mail discussion) uses language that is different from the language used by the person looking for information, it is hard to connect the artifact (and its creator) with its seeker. Technology alone cannot solve this problem, but you can solve it by making use of yet another type of managed knowledge—**taxonomies**—to provide a common framework of concepts (and relations between these concepts) to structure the lexical elements of language.

The goal of a corporate taxonomy is not only to provide a list of authorized terms for use in writing and in information seeking, but also to create maps between concepts to connect employees with the right knowledge at the right time. The taxonomies create a common semantic network that is based on business needs and takes into account the intellectual assets (the content) and the way in which the knowledge workers (the employees) look for information. Such a network provides an essential tool for managing intellectual capital and connecting employees with knowledge.

---

1. *http://www.tfpl.com/areas_of_expertise/taxonomies/_report_/taxonomy_report.html.*

In this chapter we will explore the various types of taxonomies, what their purposes are, and how they fit in a larger ecosystem of content and people. We will also address the mechanics of building and structuring your own taxonomies: where to start, how to make use of your data, and how to plan for the long haul. Finally, we will look at some of the steps that go beyond searching and content management and how you can begin to measure the success and benefit of taxonomy management in your enterprise.

What Is a Taxonomy?

What comes to mind when you think of the word taxonomy? Is it an ordered list or hierarchy of terms, possibly on the model of botanical names: kingdom, phylum, class, order, family, genus, species? Ironically, there is no agreed-upon definition for the term taxonomy or for the elements that compose it. For the purposes of this chapter, we will use the term *taxonomy* inclusively to refer to any classified collection of elements.

Although the art of taxonomy and the resulting forms of taxonomic structures are rooted in the works of Aristotle, Linnaeus, and Darwin, the meaning of the term taxonomy has been expanded to cover new purposes. We now use taxonomies for creating **metadata,** or common words to describe an object, for information retrieval, categories supporting browse navigation, schemas governing Web page layout and structure, and data control lists used in support of **data mining** (searching thousands of data records to uncover patterns and relationships contained within the activity and history store to fulfill a reporting request). Examples of these **classification** systems and the resulting taxonomies vary in structure, composition, and purpose, but they are all organized according to defined principles.

Many organizations struggle with how to provide access to **semistructured information** (information that is organized—perhaps stored in a systematic way in group files or on company servers) and **unstructured information** (possibly stored on personal hard disks or on local servers according to the desires or needs of individuals). Integration and access are difficult. Taxonomies provide the link between the knowledge workers and the content, or at least they facilitate that linking in the ways described in the sections that follow.

Descriptive Taxonomies

One type of taxonomy found in the corporate environment supports information retrieval through searching. By developing and maintaining a core set of controlled vocabularies, a company can consistently label or **tag** its content with descriptive metadata selected from these authorized vocabularies. In addition, vocabularies can capture knowledge worker terminology and map it to a company's preferred terms. A product may have an array of different names during its lifetime—for example, *N-Acetyl-p-aminophenol, Acetamidophenol, Acetaminophen,* and finally the commercial form, *Tylenol.* A knowledge worker looking for information on a product might search by a code name, a project name, a legal name, an acronym, or a common name. Active mining of new terms and phrases from emerging content and from search query logs will help keep a descriptive taxonomy relevant to the users of that information. A taxonomy built on the **thesaurus model** (designating a preferred or authorized term with entry terms or variants) helps to link these different terms together. At search time, the term that the knowledge worker uses is associated with the preferred (or key) term for more precise searching, or the knowledge worker's term is expanded to include the variant forms of the term as well as the authorized term for a broader search. Taxonomies built on the thesaurus model do not force all work groups to use a common set of terminology.

When used along with a search engine, **query term expansion**, as this synonym process is called, can reduce the amount of descriptive tagging that is required, since the tags need to contain only the term's preferred form. Used judiciously, query term expansion can improve search engine recall; that is, a larger amount of information will be gathered in response to the knowledge worker's query because the search terms are more inclusive. The point is that taxonomy of this type is *linked to content* and is *descriptive of that content* in its application.

Creating this type of taxonomy involves reviewing entries against an established set of terms and looking for similarities, differences, affinities, and dependencies. As an example, think of a sales and marketing division. Employees might use the terms *promotional materials* and *advertising materials* interchangeably, at least in informal speech. But perhaps the division's formal preference is for *advertising materials.* A solid taxonomy would include both of these terms, because users may use either in a search. But because *advertising materials* is the preferred term, it can be treated as metadata and applied through tagging to pieces of content, such as Web pages, that do not use that specific wording but really are *about* advertising materials. If someone then searched for *promotional materials,* the search would be expanded to include the preferred term, and the search would succeed.

Navigational Taxonomies

A second type of taxonomy is aimed at discovering information through browsing. Once again the taxonomy provides a controlled vocabulary, but rather than using it in the background for manipulating queries, you can display this taxonomy to knowledge workers to help them find the information they need. The navigational taxonomy consists of labels applied to categories of content based on knowledge workers' mental models of how the information is organized. Web directory services such as on the Search page of Microsoft Network (MSN)(*http://search.msn.com/*), HomeAdvisor (*http://homeadvisor.msn.com/*), and the knowledge index described in Chapter 7, "Capturing Your Organization's Knowledge Assets," are all examples of navigational taxonomies.

A navigational taxonomy is based on user behavior and not on content. As a result, the category labels may be organized differently from the concept-based descriptive taxonomy, and they also may contain words or phrases that would not meet the standards of a descriptive taxonomy. As an example, you might use a phrase like *Sell Your House* to label a set of content on the Home Advisor service on MSN. The phrase is commonly understood, but it is not concise enough for a descriptive taxonomy. How to develop a navigational taxonomy will be discussed below, but the point to remember is that a navigational taxonomy is different from a descriptive taxonomy—as we will discuss below, its role is different, it can have different rules, and the sources used to build it vary.

Creating this type of taxonomy involves determining proper information groupings for the content. These categories are managed by a business owner who is familiar with the users of that site. Let us consider human resources information as an example. We know that *dental benefits* is a type of benefit. We would make *benefits* the grouping and place *dental benefits* as a subset of that group. When the navigational taxonomy is displayed to the user, *dental benefits* appears hierarchically below *benefits,* which shows the user that the company includes dental benefits as part of the benefit package.

Another fundamental difference between descriptive and navigational taxonomies is that navigational taxonomies are often specialized and unique to an instance of information presentation (a portal, a site, an intranet), and multiple content management systems do not typically reuse them as they would a descriptive taxonomy. Navigational taxonomies are therefore not governed by the same rules about which taxonomy terms can be changed.

Data Management Vocabulary

A third type of taxonomy that is valuable in a business setting is the **data management vocabulary**. This taxonomy is a short list of authorized terms without any hierarchical structure that is used to support business transactions. For example, with a large sales force, it is most efficient if salespeople report their work using the same list of activities. They may count their contacts with companies according to a simple list of contact types (managers, decision-makers, and so on), and they may categorize the businesses they work with according to different controlled descriptors that have to do with the business's size or market. In this case, a shared taxonomy will help to support reporting needs of management and other salespeople trying to mine the information in the future. Without a shared taxonomy, a company risks developing islands of data that cannot be shared or easily utilized by the rest of the organization.

Until recently, this type of taxonomy, used for data management, had been considered separate from the descriptive taxonomy, used for content management. But there are areas of overlap. For example, if your organization decides on a geographic model of your markets (such as Europe, Asia, Africa, North America, South America, and Australia), the taxonomy used for reporting data and the taxonomy for accessing content should be the same. Besides providing a consistent user experience, sharing a taxonomy for two different purposes avoids duplication of effort, thus saving time and money.

How Taxonomies Play a Role in Content

Taxonomies are not static documents that are locked away for safekeeping. They adapt and change, just as they influence content and knowledge workers to adapt and change. In an ideal KM solution, taxonomies are interactive.

What content is created and acquired is based on the information that an organization's knowledge workers (such as its employees or customers) need. You create the taxonomy according to the content. The way knowledge workers look for information also influences the taxonomy. Values, or terms, from the taxonomy are applied to content. Values from the taxonomy are applied to knowledge worker data (such as in Active Directory service or in an employee database) so that content and expertise can be found and delivered to knowledge workers. The following sections describe these interactions more fully.

Information Needs Drive Content

A company's collection of information is dynamic, often created and managed through multiple channels and systems, and it reflects the priorities and needs of the employees, managers, and customers. The needs of the knowledge workers drive the expansion of the body of corporate information. For example, when Microsoft decided to enter the video gaming console market with Xbox, its corporate information needs grew to include competitive analyses, sales forecasting, and technology areas in the gaming market.

To identify your organization's information needs, you should first do a **needs assessment**. This analysis is similar to the organizational needs analysis suggested in Chapter 3, "Knowledge and the Business Culture," but in this case you focus on the areas of information needed to run your business. Search query logs, analysis of library reference requests, focus group results, findings from in-person interviews of individual knowledge workers, and survey results are all indicators of what content each segment of employees needs, and on what schedule. These sources also tell you about the knowledge workers' information-seeking behavior, which in turn lets you know which access methods (such as searching and browsing) and access points (such as metadata elements) you need to use in schemas and in descriptive and navigational taxonomies.

Content Informs the Taxonomy

Which concepts and terms that an enterprise should manage in a corporate taxonomy are determined by the enterprise's business needs. The aim is not to manage *all* terms but to identify which subset of terms should be included and managed. The needs analysis method described above determines what *content* needs to be created or acquired, and this same process—and the content that results—provides the scope for the taxonomy management process. This helps to determine the taxonomy's scope.

Once you know the taxonomy's scope, you can harvest new terms and concepts from existing and emerging content. The goal of this step is twofold:

- To keep the concepts in a corporate taxonomy current and synchronized with the evolving flow of created and published content
- To see that the associated terms reflect the language that the content authors use

Information-Seeking Behavior Influences Taxonomy

The differences between a navigational taxonomy and a descriptive taxonomy have already been described. When you match the taxonomy to knowledge workers' information-seeking behavior, consider the needs of navigational browsing behavior as well as searching behavior. For searching to truly support information discovery, general exploratory searches need to be as successful as the more focused known item searches, matching the entire corporate body of knowledge, the knowledge worker, and the types of information being sought.

Similarly, one of the aims of KM is not only to connect knowledge workers with knowledge and an organization's knowledge assets but also to help inform the knowledge worker in situations where appropriate content is *not* available. A KM system should not only inform the user that his or her search failed but also provide a way to give feedback to the taxonomy administrators. User feedback about failed searches informs the taxonomy administrators of the users' search selection. Taxonomy research will be needed to determine if changes to the structure or taxonomy will be needed in the future to avoid failed searches. The corporate taxonomy should include the language that is employed by the knowledge worker to describe concepts, whether or not content covers these concepts. In this manner, a KM system can not only inform the knowledge worker of the *existence* of content but also can begin to inform the knowledge worker, and the content owners, of the *lack* of content.

Taxonomy Values Are Applied to Content

Once you have a taxonomy, you can start using it to describe and categorize your organization's content. Using a taxonomy in this way supports searching, browsing, and content management. In most situations you can directly apply the terms from taxonomies to content by using metadata tags or by adding properties to the content files. An example of direct application is the use of the <META> tag from the Hypertext Markup Language (HTML) 4.01 specification placed directly into HTML content:

<META name="keywords" content="knowledge management, information discovery, taxonomies">

You can also apply metadata indirectly by storing the values separate from the content with a pointer to the content. Content registries, metadata registries, and library catalogs are examples of this type of indirect application. In both methods, content is segmented, collocated, classified, managed for timeliness, or distributed according to reliable, consistent metadata selected from a common taxonomic source.

Document management systems (such as Microsoft SharePoint Portal Server) can also provide a way to store metadata about the content—and the content itself—within the same system. In these systems, the metadata and the content are distinct and separate, but the system can intelligently index them as a single virtual document to improve retrieval through searching.

Taxonomy Values Are Applied to Knowledge Workers

A taxonomy can also be useful when it comes to information about your employees. You can use even very basic directory-level information (such as an employee's job title or work group) to dynamically display personalized information through a Web portal, team site, collaborative community, or other business application. For example, either a technical white paper or a high-level product overview could be highlighted in search results depending on a searcher's job.

You can also capture and make use of an even deeper level of knowledge worker information to provide richer features and business intelligence over the long term. For example, in a community of practice (CoP), by having a more robust profile of each participant (gathered either through implicit data mining or through explicit knowledge worker-supplied data and stored in a directory or user-profile database), a business application can provide the community participants with better information about the source and quality of the knowledge that is being presented. When a community member comes upon some information posted by a community expert, for example, he or she could find out how many solutions (in contrast to questions) that the expert has provided, the reuse rate for his or her contributions, how long he or she has been a member of that community, and what other communities he or she belongs to. In a larger context, this information can help people identify individuals with expertise in various areas across communities.

See Also   For more information about CoPs, see Chapter 5, "Creating and Sustaining Communities of Practice."

Similarly, you can capture and consolidate a knowledge worker's searching behavior (such as the order in which he or she generally requests information) and other implicit knowledge (such a current job or project) as part of that knowledge worker's profile. The exact terms that a knowledge worker enters in a search, for example, can be helpful in building a taxonomy. Then you can tag the knowledge worker with metadata to identify that person to other system users, or "push" (send information) to him or her based on what the system believes the person will want to see.

See Also   For more information about expertise finding, see Chapter 10, "Knowledge Searching and Services."

Content Is Found and Delivered to Knowledge Workers

Taxonomies can improve search engine recall in cases where queries are manipulated. For example, when a knowledge worker types a common misspelling, the taxonomy can modify the query to use the correct or authorized spelling. Taxonomies can also improve search engine precision in cases where tagging supports content registries of high-value selected content. For example, Microsoft's Knowledge Network Group maintains a registry database of "Best Bets" (with regard to search results—not the quality of the content as discussed later in Chapter 7) that represent the best information sources for a select set of common user queries. When a knowledge worker enters a general query that returns several hundred hits (a Microsoft product name, for example), the best answers for the worker's questions will appear as Best Bets at the top of the results list. Both of these enhancements save time for knowledge workers. In addition, they aid in finding the right information and, in the case of the content registry, they help to push authoritative, consistent information to the top.

A navigational taxonomy in particular brings special benefits to knowledge workers. The exposed structure of a navigational taxonomy provides employees with visual cues about an information domain's scope, as demonstrated in Figure 6-1. It gives quick access to often-used information, and it shows a sequence of steps or gives a priority order to complex information.

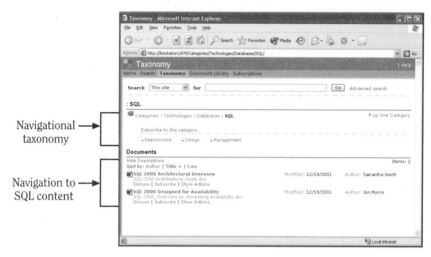

Navigational taxonomy →

Navigation to → SQL content

Figure 6-1. *Navigational Taxonomy*

Identifying Experts in the Organization

As your base of information about your employees grows, your ability to identify the expertise of the people in your enterprise will also grow. When you have information about an individual's browsing, searching, and posting habits; metadata from the content that he or she has created; the projects that he or she has worked on; community involvement; and preferences and patterns in the data he or she accesses in the corporate intranet, your portal or KM system can manage and describe the knowledge worker's experience base in the same way it shows the contents of the repository.

Capturing such information within the organization may be less controversial than doing it in an external Internet environment. But the corporate culture will likely influence or constrain the reaction to (and acceptance of) gathering, mining, manipulating, storing, and making use of what may be regarded as "my personal" information. Nevertheless, this approach can be one of the best ways of connecting employees with other employees and for the corporation to begin to learn more about the implicit knowledge that its employees have.

Building and Maintaining a Taxonomy

Taxonomy building needs to be targeted and strategic. If your world consists of a finite set of knowledge workers, products, activities, geographies, partners, and so on, build for that set with a watchful eye on the rest of the world. Maintaining a taxonomy is an oft-overlooked requirement and an underestimated cost. In planning, you should give equal consideration to what is required to build and to maintain a taxonomy or set of taxonomies.

What Do You Have Already?

As a starting point, take an inventory of any existing taxonomies. Reusing existing taxonomies can help save time and effort. Are there already established authority lists such as market segmentations, customer types, and geographies? Does your company already have a subject or keyword list that supports the library or other cataloging or publishing efforts? How widely adopted are any existing authority lists? Are there publicly available, or available for purchase, well-formed taxonomies or thesauri that would be relevant to your business information? For example, there are well-developed taxonomies for information retrieval in the areas of law, pharmacy, engineering, and ecology. Reviewing the external offerings, as well as the existing internal sources of taxonomy, will give you a solid starting point and ideas about the taxonomy's needs for granularity and scope.

Obtaining the Information

To build and maintain a reflective, strategic, targeted taxonomy, you need to seek relevant information about your organization.

Information from Knowledge Workers

As a starting point for building a core set of search vocabularies, examine search behavior as it is reflected in query logs. Query logs show the types of information that employees seek, the terms that they use, and common misspellings. With analysis over time, you will be able to determine which terms recur either constantly (such as *maps* or *Brittany*) or in a cycle (such as *taxes* or *annual meeting*).

Another source of information on knowledge worker information-seeking is feedback or problem report logs. Terminology can be at the root of problems in accessing information—did someone not find the information simply because of the way it was labeled or categorized? Focus groups, contextual interviews, and usability reports are also good sources of terminology-related information.

A formal information needs assessment, as discussed earlier in this chapter, can also help you prioritize your taxonomy-building efforts. By surveying knowledge workers to learn the most important and also the most difficult information to find, you can narrow the target and establish success metrics. Survey questions might include the following:

- What were you looking for?
- What is the ideal content you would like to have found?
- How important is this content to your job/business?

Information from Content

A well-formed taxonomy not only reflects knowledge worker needs, but it also reflects the content it organizes. There are various approaches to building the taxonomy according to content. As a starting point to determine the current use of metadata and terminology, it is valuable to undertake an audit of existing metadata tags. In Microsoft's Knowledge Network Group, metadata uncovered in a corporate-wide Web search is used to chart the use of metadata over time. In addition, a tag audit can expose a common set of metadata elements that are widely used. You might discover departments where metadata tags were in place in the documents, probably due to shared publishing tools or schemas, but were not actively used—no values had been assigned.

Content owners and stakeholders also provide a valuable, if sometimes biased, overview of content. By engaging content owners, you can draw upon their subject expertise to find out if the *right* information is being discovered and utilized. Because most content owners want to have their content highlighted in a search, you should assess their opinions in light of what you know about knowledge workers. On the other hand, content experts are in the best position to determine the strengths and weaknesses of content discovery in their domains.

See Also   You can find more information on visual mapping in Chapter 7.

See Also   For more information on measuring content, see Chapter 8, "Building a KM Foundation," and Chapter 9, "Measuring the Effectiveness of Your Repository."

Automated document analysis is a method for allowing content to guide taxonomy creation. Word counts and automated subject analyses can provide good information about the types of documents that are in your information store, the most common topics within those documents, emerging terminologies, and the like.

With database clustering technologies, like those found in Microsoft SQL Server 2000 Analysis Services, you can uncover patterns of term variants in query logs. For example, if the term *company store* is at the top of the query log list and *maps* is somewhere slightly lower on the log, a cluster analysis might find that there are, in fact, many instances where people searched for variant terms such as *map, campus maps,* and so on. By analyzing the clusters, you can determine the relative importance of the concepts, not just the search strings.

Taxonomy creation can fall anywhere along a spectrum, from being an entirely human endeavor to a fully automated project. Ideally, automated assistance can improve efficiency when handling large amounts of material. Computers are very good at finding patterns—human analysis to find the significance of those patterns can help the taxonomy grow, supporting searching as well as browsing.

Structuring the Taxonomy

Once you have determined the appropriate extent of the taxonomy effort, it is time to determine your taxonomy's structure and implementation. A taxonomy's structure can range from simple to complex. It can be a simple alphabetical listing of authorized forms of terms and phrases, also known as an authority list or flat list. It can have a more complicated structure that comes from the creation of hierarchical and associative relationships between terms. Books, online guides, consultants, and examples show options for taxonomy implementation. Both the American National Standards Institute (ANSI) and the International Organization for Standardization (ISO) have established standards and guidelines for developing and managing thesauri.[2] Because these standards were publicly announced before the impact of the Internet,

---

2. Guidelines for the Construction, Format and Management of Monolingual Thesaurus, ANSI Standard Z39.19-1993, ISO2788, ISO5964, BS5723, BS6723.

professional groups are working on updating or supplementing these standards to reflect today's digital reality.

Business needs and rules must guide decisions about management and scope, but these standards give you a solid starting point for basic decisions about forms of terms, display of terms, and structure. Even if you have several taxonomies and unique guidelines for each one, you should also have a core set of rules grounded in standards. When each taxonomy complies with established standards, you will improve the chances that they will interoperate with other groups' efforts both internally and externally.

You have many choices for storage and management of your taxonomy. These depend on specifics of your business:

- **Use.**   Is the taxonomy a list to be used in a navigation menu, a drop-down list, or a large taxonomy to support information retrieval?

- **Size.**   Will the completed taxonomy contain several terms or several thousand terms and relationships?

- **Complexity.**   Will the taxonomy be a flat list or a hierarchical structure with a number of different types of relationships linking the terms?

- **Scope of use.**   Is the taxonomy used only locally or is it shared over the enterprise or even internationally?

In simple cases (such as a small, slowly changing taxonomy that supports browsing on one Web site), you can handle storage and management with an XML file stored on the Web server. If you maintain taxonomies that change quickly, require shared management and change control, or are highly structured, you will need to invest in support processes and systems. Depending on resources, you can either purchase taxonomy management software or build a custom management solution that fits your specific needs.

A taxonomy management software solution is convenient because you do not have to build the solution from scratch and you can often integrate it into larger document warehousing solutions with minimal fuss. But a software solution is not always as flexible. Because you did not build it, some of your specialized needs may not be met by an off-the-shelf solution. You may have some ability to automatically generate new taxonomies, but these rarely meet all your needs. And when the solution is integrated into a larger document warehousing solution, you might be limited in how well the solution interacts with your existing systems.

If you decide not to buy a third-party solution, you can build your own from scratch. The primary advantage of developing your own is that you can design the system to evolve with your needs. But in-house development requires you to have the development resources and taxonomy experts.

Microsoft's Knowledge Network Group investigated several third-party taxonomy management tools before deciding to design and build its own for the management of descriptive and navigational taxonomies, as well as for metadata schemas. A design was constructed to reflect the project's goals and was built using Microsoft SQL Server. The design that was developed allows for an easily extensible structure (both in depth of hierarchy and in the types of relationships that could be supported). A Microsoft Visual Basic interface (later named VocabMan) was used so that the taxonomists, or information professionals with a keen understanding of taxonomic rules and usage, could manipulate and maintain the structures. Microsoft's Content Development and Delivery Group (CDDG) has since expanded and supplanted this solution with a similar database structure developed as an XML Web service with a Web-based management interface. It functions as a single management service for taxonomies in support of many of Microsoft's external and internal content management systems.

See Also   For additional information on XML Web services, see Chapter 10.

Managing the Taxonomy

At Microsoft, content management for internal content is distributed among many organizations. Taxonomy creation is also distributed. As in many large companies, with multiple product lines, there exists a growing movement within Microsoft to adopt a common set of vocabularies, a common core schema, and a common management system. This is desirable because it allows the knowledge workers to be more effective in searching across the company; it also reduces expensive, redundant efforts. The shared development of taxonomy, however, means that change control measures need to be in place to keep vocabularies in sync and to keep pace with the rapid growth of products and services. For example, if a term (or a group of terms) is going to be removed, all parts of the organization using that term need to be notified so that they can make appropriate changes to their publishing and data management tools. Likewise, when content owners suggest new terms, they are referred to a taxonomy committee or advisory board to decide how to add and structure the new elements within the shared taxonomy.

Centralization or Decentralization

Once you have made decisions about your taxonomy's scope and implementation, you still have to decide how to manage it. Keeping the management model small has practical advantages. Having a centralized, dedicated group working together to build and manage a taxonomy saves time and effort. Building vocabularies by committee is tedious and wastes energy. On the other hand, even the best group of expert taxonomists will need constant input from content owners to keep abreast of new information needs that drive a vital taxonomy. An advisory panel can represent the needs of different groups cooperating on the taxonomy.

Microsoft's model utilizes both a centralized and decentralized taxonomy. Administrators work toward sharing a core set of controlled vocabularies but also recognize that the groups they work with have different needs for specific topical coverage and management schemas. To that end, Microsoft builds out shared vocabularies but saves room for groups to manage their own local term sets.

Balancing centralized control with the reality of distributed management can be difficult, but without some centralized control there is no consistency, and the taxonomy's strength is undermined. Unlike many other shared goals or KM initiatives, the corporate taxonomy really does need to be a unique, shared effort at its core. As with industry standards, a shared taxonomy leads to interoperability—which is highly desirable in a distributed work environment. At the very least, it is important to standardize a single taxonomy approach that is supported by agreed-upon standards. It is also desirable to work toward a shared taxonomy platform for the same reasons: interoperability and elimination of redundant efforts.

Authority and Support

As mentioned earlier, controling change is vital to the ongoing success of a shared taxonomy. It is crucial to stay in sync and informed of changes. By having a built-in advisory group across the company that pushes for taxonomy changes, all corners of the organization benefit from hearing about changes in a timely way and having them reflected in their shared taxonomy. It is important to determine from the start who has a voice in making change control decisions. It is also desirable to set up in advance the rules on who is responsible for implementing changes.

In cases where the need to be stable outweighs the need to be current, a scheduled update approach to making vocabulary changes can help to moderate the impact of changes to the taxonomy. In this case, you accumulate change requests, a representative group reviews them, and you make changes to the taxonomy quarterly or according to some other appropriate schedule. This scheduled updating of the taxonomy allows the central authority to give plenty of warning to the knowledge workers. This approach makes sense in cases where taxonomy changes necessitate related work such as updated documentation. This cascade of change within an organization often requires lead time.

Another approach is to make real-time changes in taxonomy—that is, agreed-upon changes are immediately effective rather than implemented on a scheduled basis. This method requires well-established change control rules governing what kind of changes can occur without notice (adding vocabulary, updating spelling, and so on) and what kind of changes require notice or even consensus among a broader group of knowledge workers or the advisory panel (deleting terms or vocabularies, radical restructuring, and so on).

In addition to balancing the business needs of different groups that use the taxonomy, change control rules need to account for the impact of reorganizations and other changes in the company. By initially structuring who owns the business rules and change control decisions, the taxonomy updating process can continue without interruption. To withstand changes in the organization, a good set of taxonomy change control rules will also codify how to change the rules when necessary.

Ongoing Maintenance

As you allocate resources for the maintenance of the taxonomy, determine whether tagging or other content management will be centralized or distributed. If use of the taxonomy is distributed, you will need to set a training budget. If the process is centralized, you will need to hire content managers. In either case, you will need to hire taxonomists to manage the taxonomy, work through change control, and keep the contents up to date. Also, determine whether any or all of the work can be outsourced.

Microsoft outsources much of the tagging, and occasionally brings in temporary staff or consultants to help meet project deadlines, but the majority of the work on taxonomy development and maintenance is done by full-time staff.

Being Strategic

Throughout the description of planning and implementing the taxonomy, we have provided suggestions on how to keep your efforts targeted toward the biggest returns. Here is a summary:

- Review knowledge worker behavior to find out where the needs and use are greatest

- Analyze content to determine scope and depth
- Reflect business priorities in your taxonomy
- Develop and implement a scaleable solution, leaving room for future development, and allocate resources for maintenance and growth
- Establish a metrics plan that can help you determine what is going well and what can be changed to maximize your effectiveness

Using Taxonomies to Their Fullest

The obvious strengths of corporate taxonomies have already been described; they include search support, navigation, data control/mining, schema management, and personalization/information delivery. But the value of a taxonomy does not stop there. With the infrastructure of a shared set of controlled vocabularies, you can take advantage of other benefits.

A taxonomy can become a part of content creation itself. For example, in the airplane manufacturing industry, it is critical to control vocabulary for consistency and precision in instructions and manuals. In this case the technical writers use the terminology contained in the controlled taxonomy to create the instructions and manuals. The controlled terminology is now part of the full-text content, and users of these documents can be confident that they have been applied consistently and precisely.

When taxonomy is used in support of document tagging, the taxonomy can become part of the content creation/tagging process. In a company with many content creation channels and methods, a centralized corporate taxonomy can feed directly into a content management system, into stand-alone tagging tools, or into any other method used to tag content. The benefit of having all the different methods draw upon the same centralized taxonomy is consistent tagging and normalization, along with a simplification of the tagging process.

Controlled vocabularies also provide a stable foundation for localization. Once the vagaries of one language have been reduced to describe a single concept, the ability to use this structure for translation into other languages is obvious.

Taxonomies often bring valuable by-products. For example, a corporate taxonomy will likely contain abbreviations. If the taxonomy is structured in a way that allows the retrieval of elements by their relationship type, it is a simple matter to create an resource that shows the meaning or meanings of abbreviations and acronyms. Similarly, code names, language codes, and other lists can be pulled from the centrally maintained source.

Finally, and perhaps most importantly, a taxonomy can help to ensure that knowledge workers are seeing the right, consistent information. Taxonomies can help to make obvious the authoritative sources of information, and they can help prioritize information for knowledge workers within search returns and by directing navigation.

Measuring Success

How do you know that your taxonomy is working? It can be difficult to determine which performance or satisfaction gains are directly attributable to taxonomy. Depending on how you take advantage of your taxonomy, you may try the following methods to measure success:

Relevancy testing.   As mentioned earlier, if your taxonomy is used to enhance searching, relevancy testing (the precision and recall measures familiar from information retrieval studies) is a good indicator of success. If you use taxonomies to manipulate search queries and search result sets, you can improve both precision and recall and you can retrieve more relevant information.

Item reuse.   Another measure of navigation and search efficiency is that authoritative information is reused. You can monitor this using corporate intranet site statistics. By noting the position of the search result selected by knowledge workers, you can determine the effectiveness of content registries and the taxonomies that support them. When knowledge workers find high-quality information in the top three search results, they seldom go deeper into the list, and the authoritative, tagged items are reused.

Usability testing.   This is a valuable way to test navigational taxonomy. Are knowledge workers able to find common resources quickly? Can you reduce the time to complete a task by improving the labeling of categories? Contextual methods, where knowledge workers' search behaviors are observed in their offices, can also show qualitative gains related to both navigation and search taxonomies.

Knowledge worker satisfaction.   Survey results are a reliable metric only when they can be narrowed to focus on the taxonomies. If you ask knowledge workers about a search, they may base their responses on their satisfaction (or dissatisfaction) with the search results rather than on the search functionality. Other variables, such as the user interface or reaction to change, also influence knowledge workers' satisfaction with searching and browsing.

Summary

Once you have metrics in place, you can decide how effective your taxonomy implementation is in context. At the same time, it is valuable to take a more holistic approach and review some checkpoints of a good taxonomy.

- An effective taxonomy is extensible over time. Mergers and acquisitions will not destroy the model, nor will changes in the organization that affect the maintenance of the taxonomy.

- Rules concerning taxonomy management focus on what is similar among knowledge workers and find a way to keep dissimilar goals from sidetracking the project.

- A well-reasoned corporate taxonomy management system ought to be, to the greatest extent possible, independent of the systems in which the resultant taxonomies will be leveraged. This builds in flexibility for future use.

- A vital taxonomy is tightly connected to content producers in order to keep up to date and to reflect both the organizational and the individual knowledge workers' information needs.

- A strategic taxonomy accounts for business priorities and keeps a focus on and measures how to continually have the most beneficial effect on the evolving information environment.

Proper planning and management of a corporate taxonomy strategy should be the cornerstone of any KM effort. If it is ignored, processes for managing terms and structures evolve organically and emerge without a unifying vision. Recovering from such a situation will be an even greater challenge. By identifying the goals of your KM efforts and how taxonomies can support them and by being strategic in your approach, you can begin to build a system of structures that will grow with your enterprise and that will continue to support your KM needs.

Establish common vocabulary

Connect people to content

Capturing Your Organization's Knowledge Assets

I not only use all the brains I have, but all I can borrow.

Woodrow Wilson (1856–1924),
Twenty-eighth President of the United States

In Chapter 6, "Building Taxonomies," we discussed the benefit of having a taxonomy—a system for tagging and categorizing knowledge assets—so that content can be easily searched. In this chapter we extend this concept to explain methods of collecting, organizing, and sharing content based on your taxonomy. We identify types of knowledge assets and show you how to select content your organization needs based on your taxonomy. We will also review some methods you can use to keep track of your content and expose those assets to internal and external audiences.

Historically, the term **intellectual property (IP)** has been used to define a variety of documents. The U.S. Patent Office defines IP as "... imagination made real. It is the ownership of dreams, an idea, an improvement, an emotion that we can touch, see, hear, and feel. It is an asset just like your home, your car, or your bank account."[1] In this chapter we will use the term **knowledge assets (KAs)** to describe all the forms of collected knowledge, including IP, that an organization's repository contains. We will use KA in the broadest sense to include such things as project plans, architectural diagrams, meeting transcripts, code samples, and formal and informal documentation. A KA is any learned information owned by an individual or a knowledge-creating company.

---

1. U.S. Patent Office. *What is Intellectual Property? http://www.uspto.gov/web/offices/ac/ahrpa/ opa/museum/intell.html.* (Washington, D.C., 1998).

Knowledge Asset Role

KAs come from a variety of sources in an organization—product development groups, marketing, employees, and management. Getting the right content to the right audience is the goal of any knowledge management (KM) program. How a KA is presented depends on the audience that uses and reuses it.

In Chapter 1, "Knowledge Is the Foundation of Business," we defined the Knowledge Cycle and demonstrated how knowledge moves through the four quadrants of creation (Personal, Community, Corporate, and Public). Our next step is to look at the role of KAs in the Knowledge Cycle. In Figure 7-1, you can see that each quadrant handles and presents knowledge to diverse audiences in slightly different ways. In the Personal Knowledge Space, the KA is owned, or controlled, by the individual. In the Community Knowledge Space, the community shares KAs—that is, community members may share in creating, reviewing, and reusing the KA. In the Corporate Knowledge Space, all corporate employees use KAs; in most cases the corporation has staff who create and edit formal documents to be used by the company knowledge workers. In the last quadrant, the Public Knowledge Space, the corporation releases KAs for both employees and the public to view and use.

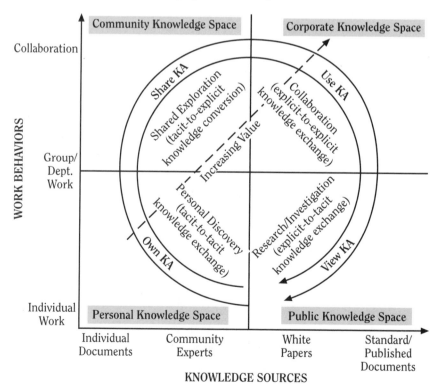

Figure 7.1.   *Knowledge Cycle and Roles of Knowledge Assets*

In the Knowledge Cycle we see how KAs are owned, shared, used, and viewed by the different audiences (members of the community) in each quadrant. Although knowledge may be handled differently in each quadrant (responsibilities may be shared or be passed to others), the underlying flow of creating, managing, and publishing is the same in all four knowledge spaces.

Flow of Knowledge

As they flow from being dispersed to being collected, organized, and shared with others, KAs take a generally established path, as Figure 7-2 demonstrates.

Step	Personal Space	Community Space	Corporate Space	Public Space
1 Knowledge Development	Customer Call Incident Report	Call Center Incident Report	KB Record	KB Editors
2 Content Management	Local Server	Services Tracking Database	KB System	Web Content or Product Book
3 Knowledge Exposure	Incident Record Screen	Tracking Screen	KB Screens	Published Articles

Figure 7-2.   *Implementing the Flow of Knowledge*

The first step in knowledge development is the creation of the knowledge itself. The knowledge development layer converts tacit knowledge—that is, what a person knows—into a written form identified as a KA. A good illustration of converting tacit knowledge into a written explicit form is the Knowledge Base (KB) system used by Microsoft's Product Support Service (PSS) group. A PSS support engineer (SE) enters an incident into the incident tracking system as he or she talks to a customer about product problems or issues. The SE then researches the issue and reports the solution back to the customer. The solution is generally information derived from conversations with other SEs or consultants or is found in previous incident records in the KB. The solution, once discovered and proven to work with the customer, can be recorded in the KB system for reuse. Hence the tacit learned information is transformed into written content and is shared and reused by PSS and other groups within Microsoft.

The second step shown in Figure 7-2 is content management of the KA in the KM library, or repository. This is where the KAs are catalogued and indexed so that members of the community (either employees or the general public) can organize and search them. Even in the Personal Space, managing content is important if you want to find your material again. Naming conventions and methods for identifying content are necessary not only to keep your house in order but also to find information in a timely manner.

Knowledge exposure is the third and final layer. This step involves passing knowledge to others or exposing it through Web sites or other mechanisms. This layer is the actual publication stage. Communities and companies generally have rules about when, where, and how material can be published or exposed to others.

See Also   You can find more information about repository tool choices in Chapter 8, "Building a KM Foundation."

All four KM spaces make use of these three layers—knowledge development, content management, and knowledge exposure.

- Individuals continually use the Personal Space, in which they create, communicate, and learn. An individual develops, manages, and exposes knowledge depending on his or her goals and work activities. KAs in the personal space can be as simple as a task or contact list or as complex as step-by-step system instructions.

- The Community Space is a group of individuals with a specific focus and set of shared goals. In this space the KA is shared only internally with other community members. This collective sharing of KAs reinforces the community's learning and strengthens the community's focus on its goals. KAs in the community space might be code samples, project specifications, or job task instructions.

- The Corporate Space reinforces the organization's mission and vision. It contains KAs that are targeted to employees and stakeholders. KAs in the Corporate Space might include the company's benefit packages, the employees' handbook, and operations details for the business. The Corporate Space is where KAs are shared internally if they are not ready for public exposure but are required for internal productivity. One such document might be an installation manual for a product that is still in development and not ready to be released to customers.

- The World Wide Web is the window to the Public Space and is the disclosure of corporate KAs to the world. KAs in the Public Space are generally edited by marketing and legal departments so that they reflect the professional and formal view of a company or community. The Public Space might contain marketing and sales literature. Semi-public space can also include business partners with whom the company shares prerelease materials.

Once KAs are developed and moved from the Personal into the Community, Corporate, or Public Space, they are generally submitted to a repository where they are stored, managed, and made available to community members, knowledge workers, and the public for reuse. The following sections discuss some of the barriers and enablers of these steps in more detail.

Capturing Knowledge Assets

A repository of useful KAs does not just magically take shape. You have to actively seek out content to build up your organization's collection of KAs. Expect to get the initial information for your repository from a variety of sources. Based on the experience of Microsoft Consulting Services in the development of its internal KM solution, it will take at least 30 days—if you have motivated participants—to build initial content in your repository.

What Compels People to Submit

The goal of the community and the goal of the business should be aligned. If your company goals are focused on selling bigger and better solutions, your communities of practice (CoPs) should concentrate on knowledge that supports that effort. One way to meet KA submission goals for a community is to reward the submission behavior by knowledge workers and managers. If you can, get managers to agree to include KM submission objectives in each participant's performance review. Review and report on the progress for knowledge workers and for each community on a quarterly basis. The submission objectives can be based on a point system in which points are awarded to the knowledge workers who create and reuse KAs. The points received should be awarded based on the level (of validation) that the submission eventually attains. Points can also be awarded for reusing KAs. The following table outlines some possible examples:

Table 7-1.   Sample Point System for KA Submissions

Level	Points	Description
Entry level	0	The status of all new content submissions.
Level 1	1	If the KA is approved by a subject matter expert in the community, the author receives points. If it does not meet community standards, it is rejected and no points are given.
Level 2	2	If the process requires two subject matter experts to review and approve the content, the maximum points are awarded and the content receives an "excellent" rating.
Level 3	4	If the content receives the status of excellent, it can be reviewed by the problem-solving organization for supportability. If it is accepted, maximum points are given to the author.
Level 4	8	If the content has passed all of the prior levels, it could be sent to an advisory board for company-wide acceptance. If approved, it will become a new standard for the company, and the author receives the maximum number of points. (It should be noted that only a small percentage of content makes its way to this level.)
Reuse	2	Points are also awarded to knowledge workers who reuse KAs from the repository and provide feedback on the KA's quality or value.

Set up the KM system to inform the managers and participants of each community of the points and objectives attained at the end of each quarter. In addition to recognizing KA submissions, community leaders and managers can use the same point scheme to reward content submissions by the knowledge worker author. Subsequently, the KA author, as well as the author's manager, should be advised of the points achieved each quarter. Rewards and recognition can be then tied to the knowledge worker's performance review at the end of the quarter.

Each community should also keep a list of "submissions wanted." If an author creates and submits content from this list, he or she can automatically receive extra points. The "submissions wanted" list can be derived from the missing KA needed to fill the community wish list. If the KA submitted is from this identified list, the author should state clearly on the submission form (perhaps by selecting a check box on the form) that the KA is being submitted to fill a requirement. Identifying needed content from the wish list gives the community leaders the ability to request specific content from the community members.

Using What You Already Have

Even if your organization does not have a formal KM solution in place, it already captures some information—employees produce business processes, products, and services every day. To start using this information, you need to identify each process and list the subjects and topics in each. Then break each topic down to performable tasks and collect the content for each aspect of the process. It is helpful to outline or map out the significant phases for each process and identify the KAs that exist for each phase, subject, topic, and task performed in the process. Also, it is recommended that you assign a subject matter expert (SME) to help identify the list of tasks and help collect content.

Another usful exercise is to conduct a needs assessment with the key stakeholders—those in the business responsible for the business objectives and the employees (anyone involved in the Knowledge Cycle) or customers. The needs assessment is based on feedback from your customer on the reliability, credibility, and ease of use of existing or future products and services.

When you start building a repository, a helpful step is to perform a gap analysis to compare what is already captured, even informally, and what still needs to be captured. A gap analysis can be an informal assessment or a formal cataloging of KAs. Once you know the content gap in your repository you can go about creating content to fill it. Depending on the culture, your organization might already have a lot of information and knowledge in personal stored files; if this is the case, your content gaps can be quickly filled.

The purpose of these assessments is to identify the content that you need and want to capture. This will assist knowledge workers who will provide the needed information. The gap analysis will identify deficiencies, and you can use them to set targets for improvement and set a measurement for success. You might find that key information for a business unit is consistently out of date or it is not entirely reliable, or that employees do not trust the information, so they do not use it in their analyses. Instead, they recreate the information themselves each time they need it. In response, you could set a target within your KM organization stating that the next time the gap analysis is done, you will score *x* percent higher in reliability and that your content will be current. If your KAs are reliable and current, you would expect employees to then spend less time recreating the data each time they reuse it. Employees can rate the content, and your SMEs and community leaders can evaluate and rate the results.

Creating a Knowledge Index

It is easy to get overwhelmed by all the content that needs to be collected for a repository. Creating a **knowledge index (KI)** can help you think about your content systematically.

A KI, similar to a table of contents, can help you identify and guide the knowledge requirements for your organization. It helps you structure content so that information is easy to recognize and find. It is best to create a KI for each community and align it to the community focus. That way the index will remain limited to the community's sphere of interest and will not become so large that it is difficult to use. The community leader and SMEs should be responsible for creating the initial index and should get input from community volunteers.

A KI helps to quickly guide employees to a specific KA that they are looking for. A supply chain KI, for example, allows members of an e-commerce consulting community to find information about designing and implementing a complete supply chain solution for their customers. To illustrate the development of a KI, consider the categories needed to define a supply chain knowledge index.

Building a supply chain KI will require hierarchically outlining the entire supply chain flow, which is similar to a book outline. The first step is to identify the major categories in the supply chain and continue to break each category down until the framework of the outline is complete, as shown in Figure 7-3. In this example the highest category—similar to a book title—is Supply Chain. "Section" titles or subheadings—Planning, Raw Materials, Manufacturing, and Distribution—divide the process of a supply chain into more manageable parts. A further division, similar to a chapter, breaks down section information into smaller classes, and topic-level categories such as Vendor Selection, Raw Material Selection, and Transportation Requirements clearly define the categories of content that a knowledge worker is seeking. The KI's purpose is to visually map the known KAs (and identify missing elements) for a specific community focus. Not all information about supply chain management will be appropriate for this community since its focus is the design, development, and implementation of e-commerce technology solutions. Each KI is a unique view of the world supported by the community building the KI.

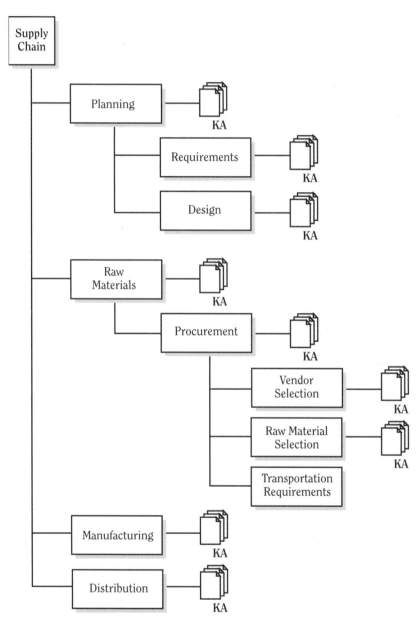

Figure 7-3.   *Example of a Supply Chain Knowledge Index*

The difficult part of constructing a KI is defining the levels that make up the structure or framework that holds the content. It helps to establish the following information about your community before starting a knowledge index:

- Determine the community's goal and focus and organize the structure in such a way that the content supports them.

- Identify the type and aspects of data to be collected for the community (white papers, case studies, code samples, and so on).

- Structure the index so that the content flows in a logical order (like a book with a title, sections, chapters, and topics of shareable knowledge content).

- Determine additional dimensions needed to round out your index. Consider the different technologies, products, and services needed to support the index.

- Identify the knowledge workers in the community and determine what knowledge they need to perform their work assignments.

Once you have a basic KI, your next step is to match the individual KAs to the index. The benefit of using a KI is that it can change quite quickly to respond to changing information or the needs of the community. KIs are dynamically constructed and can be revised and upgraded as new information or a change in direction occurs. It is only the organization of the index that remains the same.

With the KI framework built, the community can start submitting the documents, case studies, code samples, and so on that correspond to the topics defined and plug them in to the outline. Sometimes the repository already contains KAs before you create the KI. If this happens, create a KI and then perform a gap analysis between the KAs in the repository and the index topics. After you have mapped all the KAs in the repository, you may find that an abundance of KAs fills one part of the index and other parts are empty. In Figure 7-3's Supply Chain Knowledge Index, the folder Transportation Requirements contains no KAs. Auditing a repository to identify missing KAs in this way shows which new content to solicit from the community. When you know what is missing from the repository, you can prioritize the creation of new KAs.

When all the KAs are represented, you will need to revise and adapt the index as the community goals and objectives change and grow. Remember that the index holds the knowledge focus of the community; consequently, if KAs are missing, the community members will have difficulty fulfilling their work objectives.

How Microsoft Uses a Knowledge Index

Microsoft Consulting Services (MCS) designs and develops technology solutions for customers in varied industries. Its members are predominately Microsoft field-based consultants. KM in the MCS organization consists of five technology communities: Platforms, Messaging, Distributed Applications, Database, and Commerce. The focus of the five technology communities is the implementation of Microsoft technology. The MCS KM repository contains many thousands of KAs that consultants can download and reuse. As the repository grew, consultants found it harder to quickly find the exact information they wanted. Searching, even with the use of advanced search techniques, was not always effective. Consultants were often looking for complex information that related to multiple keywords. These complex queries returned hundreds of suggested KAs. Also, it was difficult for community leaders to identify which knowledge topics lacked KAs. The communities needed an alternate way to locate and organize their KAs.

The solution was to create a KI to allow the community members to visually view, in a map-like presentation, what was in the repository. Figure 7-4 shows the MCS KM Repository Knowledge Index for the Commerce community. The tree, similar to common indexed structures found in databases, contains subfolders that hold documents. Presenting users with this familiar organizational pattern will allow them to easily find documents by category and chunks of information in logical order. In Figure 7-4, some of the folders contain either more subfolders or more documents, while other folders display all content (revealing all nested folders or documents, or both) or the folder is empty. Validated KA documents are highlighted. (For additional information, see the section "Validation," later in this chapter.) By structuring the repository in expandable indexes, members can view, select, and reuse KAs in logical groupings. This also enables the community's leaders to identify missing KAs and solicit KAs from members to fill the holes.

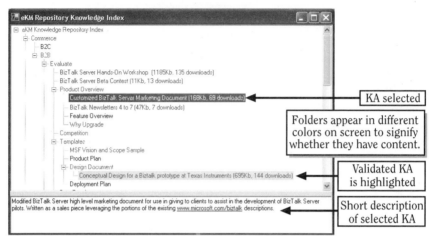

Figure 7-4.   *MCS KM Repository Knowledge Index*

Content from Communities of Practice

If your organization has CoPs, they can play a big role in adding content to your repository. That content can come from either individual community participants or SMEs, as shown in Figure 7-5.

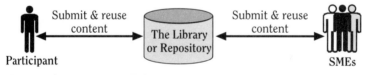

Figure 7-5.   *Repository Submission*

See Also   You can find more information about communities of practice in Chapter 5, "Creating and Sustaining Communities of Practice."

Content from Corporate and Public Web Sites

Sometimes it is important to not only collect and share internal company information, but also to share content with other corporate (but still internal) and external sites. This is usually done through an intranet or public Web site.

Capturing knowledge at the corporate or public (Web) level can take place at two different times:

- **Pre-publishing.**   Information and knowledge are identified based on a predefined set of needs. You can request that individuals or groups produce the information and share their knowledge according to a set of publishing standards. This process determines what content is shared with the audience on the Web site.

- **Post-publishing.**   Information is captured after it has been published—that is, after it has been posted on a department or group site. What is captured is defined by a Web crawler, a program that you can use to search through the World Wide Web or intranet sites, looking for pertinent topics. Web crawlers are instructed as to what content to look for by a set of keywords (also known as metadata tags). These tags are set up as part of the initialization of the Web crawler. If utilized as part of the publishing process, a Web crawler can routinely look at department and group Web sites for content of interest to the larger audience. Documents should be reviewed before they are posted on a corporate or public Web site. Key reviewing considerations when posting content for the larger audiences may include:

  - Legal reviews

  - Marketing review

  - Taxonomy tags (see Chapter 6 for more detailed information)

Knowledge capture needs to be as simple as possible. The more complicated it is, the less likely employees are going to want to contribute to or reuse it, even if they are rewarded for their KM behaviors. In a post-publishing scenario, the quality of what is delivered to the end user depends on the standards and guidelines established by the owner of the search mechanism. The search owner might work with the key or high-volume content owners or authors to establish standards. The search owner can set up a registration method that might include filters (key words that indicate appropriate returns) and measures of performance (how the content reacts when the consumer requests it).

The number of requirements depends on people's willingness or ability to participate. Reaching a larger audience rewards the author, but make sure the information is simple to use and trouble-free once a knowledge consumer downloads it.

Managing Knowledge Assets

Managing content keeps a repository's KAs fresh and vital, which helps bring the users back for repeat visits. Updating and cycling new ideas on your site gives the KM environment an innovative image. Editorial or designated content managers generally manage corporate and public repositories. These spaces are more formal in nature and are typically operated by professional writers and journalists so that the company's image is maintained. In these environments, submissions are validated through an evaluation process to ensure high-quality KAs. Content that is outdated is cycled out of the repository so that KAs remain current with product and industry advances. Managed and unmanaged community knowledge indexes change and evolve as the work objectives of the knowledge space evolve. The combined efforts of the community leader and the SMEs maintain content for the communities and the knowledge workers and staff for the Corporate and Public Spaces.

A good repository provides a solid foundation for any KM system. In Figure 7-2, Implementing the Flow of Knowledge, we saw the three layers of KM, from knowledge development, which constitutes the beginning of the cycle, to knowledge exposure, displaying the end result. In the middle is the content management layer, which contains the library or repository. Figure 7-6 is a closer look at that middle layer. Once content is entered into the system, it passes through the corporate information system—content management processes where the KAs are organized, classified, and tagged; this is also where the rules and indexing are housed to regulate the proper user community permissions.

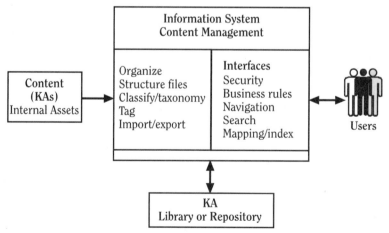

Figure 7-6. *The Library or Repository*

The community repository, as shown on the left side of Figure 7-7, includes all KAs collected, with different degrees of validation. The community repository KAs may be grouped as follows:

- Raw KAs (content created by the author and submitted to the repository)
- Validated KAs (content that has been reviewed by a SME)
- Validated KAs with supportability (content that has been validated by a SME plus reviewed by a problem-solving group, such as help desk experts)
- Best practices (content that has been reviewed by the experts in the community and declared the very best way to perform the task or procedure)

A raw KA may be a white paper or code sample produced during a project and submitted to the repository for others to reuse. A validated KA might be instructions on how to integrate different software products; this KA is reviewed, tested, and approved by a community SME. A validated KA with supportability might be an approved KA that has been tested by a support organization and is being used in procedural manuals when working with a customer repair problem, for example. Best practice KAs are usually made into standards and rules of operation for everyone in the organization to follow.

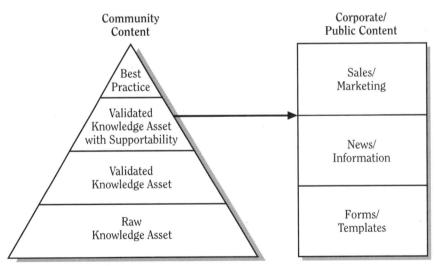

Figure 7-7. *Community, Corporate, and Public Content*

The corporate repository, shown on the right side of Figure 7-7, could contain the rules, procedures, and processes about internal products and services. The public repository might contain sales and marketing information about the corporation's products and services. Both corporate and public content can contain news flashes and can serve information and training purposes. To pass content from the community to the corporate or public repository, or both, the marketing and legal departments review the content before it can be read by employees or the public. At Microsoft, the MCS consultants frequently create product white papers, and before they are posted to a corporate or public site they go through a legal and marketing review. During this process they are edited to make sure they meet corporate standards. No set rule defines the type of content that can be admitted into a community, corporation, or public repository. The question is: what is the need of the audience? What is the appropriate levelof security and privacy that should be applied to the KA? Is this KA private and marked internal only? If so, you might consider a secured repository for this type of KA and make it accessible only to the corporation and the individual communities. Decide what the most appropriate content management guidelines are for your business and take care to validate the contents of the repository for quality, security, and privacy.

Validation

Validated KAs are the community's most valued work. Work that is reviewed and validated by experts provides accurate knowledge to others. It is intended to save the audience time (productivity gains) and the company money (efficiency gains) by providing the needed content at the right time to the right person. Anyone in the community should be able to nominate a submission (documents, presentations, code samples, case studies, other collateral, or a combination of these) for review. Content classified as validated KA should have been reviewed and approved through a published evaluation process. Published standards help to develop trust and confidence in the user community. A validated KA should have the following characteristics:

- It is highly reusable for the target audience. It represents the author's best work and renders a high degree of accuracy.
- It is validated through testing, implementation, and experience.
- It is identified as a valuable component of the knowledge index.
- It is identified as a topic that supports the goals and objectives of the community.

Each company will have its own validation rules and an evaluation process that reflect its business environment. When you set up validation rules, be fair and consistent. Set the bar high enough to maintain quality without disqualifying good content. The following are example submission requirements for validated KAs, from the MCS KM Web site:

- Where applicable, submitted content should contain a cover document that contains the following sections:

  - **Intent.**   A short statement that answers the following questions: what is the content about? what problem or issue does it address?

  - **Motivation.**   Why was this content created? Include date of creation, who used it, and who participated in the content creation.

  - **Applicability.**   In what situations will this content be useful? Provide a short scenario, if possible. Include benefits.

  - **Manifest.**   List the contents and provide a short (one-sentence) description of each of the content files or modules.

- All slides or presentation materials must come with reasonable speaker notes. A bulleted statement without proper notation guidelines can be misleading. Consequently, accompanying text clarifies the points in the slides.

- Technical documents: sample code, sample applications or process diagrams, with the following restrictions:

  - Highly Important: no sample application (which results in an executable) should be submitted as a Validated KA without simple and reliable instruction methods.

  - Sample applications must come with a corresponding document describing their use.

  - Although not required, screen shots of the application can be included to provide the reader with a sense of the application before spending the time to install it.

  - All technical sample comments should be in the audience's primary language, if possible.

- Content should be marked with the proper security level based on company policy.

Your organization's (or community's) process for validation will also differ depending on your business needs and culture. Promotion of KAs should stop when a reviewer denies the KA. (See Figure 7-8 for the processes that might apply to level reviews.) At submission and each subsequent level, the submitter and his or her manager should be sent an e-mail message containing a link to the submission and its status (with dates). The community leader should also receive a copy of the message (with reviewers' comments) for all submissions that have passed a review stage.

When an author submits KAs to the repository, he or she should be able to nominate that KA for the review process upon submission. Alternately any member should be able to nominate the content for review once it is in the repository. You might consider a five-level review cycle to evaluate KAs, as shown in Figure 7-8. The following are descriptions of the review stages in such a cycle:

Review 1	Peer reviews KA—If approved, the KA is passed to a SME for review. If rejected, the KA is sent back to the author and removed from the repository.
Review 2	SME reviews KA—If approved, the KA is awarded the status of Validated Knowledge Asset (VKA). Possibly passed on to Review 4. If rejected, the KA is sent to a second SME (Review 3) for review. Remains in the repository waiting for the second SME review.
Review 3	Second SME reviews KA—If approved, it is awarded the status of VKA. Possibly passes it on to Review 4. If rejected, the KA is sent back to the author and removed from the repository.
Review 4	Help Desk reviews VKA (reviews performed by a group of problem-solving experts)—If approved, it is awarded the status of VKA with Supportability. Possibly passes the VKA with Supportability to the Advisory Board for Best Practice review. If denied, stays as a VKA in the repository.
Review 5	Advisory Board reviews (reviews performed by a panel of SMEs and CLs) VKA with Supportability—If approved, it is awarded the Best Practice. If denied, stays as a VKA with Supportability in the repository.
	Other potential reviews might be a full legal review or a product review.

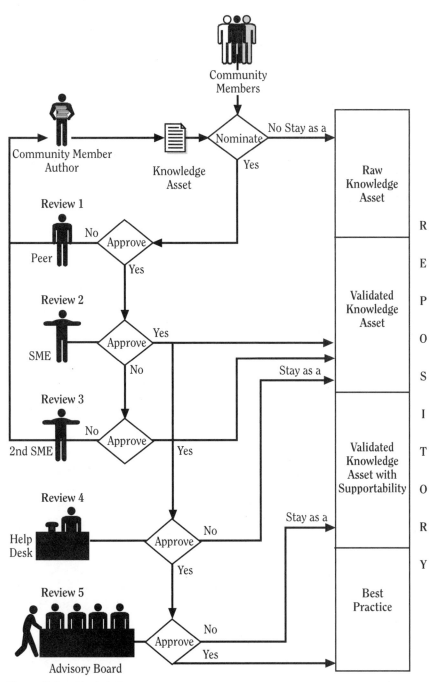

Figure 7-8.   *Review Process*

Archiving

Maintaining and managing KAs in the repository requires archiving and purging content when it no longer provides value. New product versions sometimes replace old products. In this case the KA supporting the old version should be archived so that searches for the product information will display only the new version of the product. KAs that support discontinued products or services (as dictated by the content rules of the business unit using the KM system) should usually also be purged from the repository. Support organizations are generally an exception to this rule as they often keep KAs relating to discontinued products to answer support calls. Company policies, procedures, and marketing messages change over time, and this affects content in the repository. Establish procedures for archiving and purging outdated KAs. Purging content eliminates confusion over which products and services your company is providing and the possibility of an ill-informed employee passing on incorrect information.

See Also   For information on archiving tools, See Chapter 9, "Measuring the Effectiveness of Your Repository."

Exposing Knowledge Assets to Others

As we have discussed, an organization's knowledge is most valuable when it can be reused efficiently. But before knowledge can be reused, it needs to be exposed to others. KAs can be made available to the knowledge worker or the public through a variety of methods, as discussed earlier. Your organization probably already uses basic communication tools such as e-mail, conference calls, meetings, presentations (formal and informal), and conferences to expose some KAs. Your methods of communication depend on your organization's size and complexity.

See Also   For more information about communication techniques, see Chapter 5. For more information about software tools for Web sites and home pages, see Chapter 8.

Exposing information or new content through "general broadcast" messages alerts the community members to new or important content. An updated message can save participants valuable time that they might otherwise spend searching for answers or recreating the same content. Available content is an invaluable training tool for new or inexperienced knowledge workers. Knowing where to look for content that contains the answers to your questions, and knowing that, once you find the answers, they are accurate, is fundamental to building trust and confidence in your KM environment. A KM environment should be a one-stop shopping site, so keeping your Community, Corporate, and Public Spaces focused on the original vision and scope will bring business value to your organization. If you stay true to your purpose, knowledge workers will continue to trust, use, and reuse the KAs in the repository.

To demonstrate the importance of knowledge exposure and show how KM can produce true business value, let us look at Trey Research, a fictitious mid-size business with annual revenues of approximately $150 million. Trey Research develops, manufactures, and distributes professional and commercial sound products.

Trey Research's problem was that its applications and documents were spread across too many platforms and systems. It was hard for employees to access information they needed to do their job—for example, it took so much time to find answers to customer and dealer inquiries that Trey Research was losing business to competitors. The estimated loss was growing to nearly 10 percent of its repeat business, or approximately $10 million per year. Customer satisfaction data revealed very low scores on product information availability surveys (a very poor 2 points out of a possible 10). Trey needed a way to bring order to its store of business information. The business objective was to provide easy access and distribute information contained in a wide variety of company sources. The goal was to reduce the repeat business loss in the first year by 5 percent and increase customer satisfaction with phone-in requests by two points.

The answer for Trey Research was to consolidate its team, corporate, and external information in one Web portal. The company also provided links to tools that helped employees make decisions based on business information that was collected through the portal. It created a community Web site that gave employees a central location for workgroups to share documents and contact information. This community page also served as a discussion forum for collaboration. Now instead of spending hours to access various data sources to answer and research customer and dealer issues, employees accessed relevant data with just a few keystrokes. Trey found that customer satisfaction scores did increase by more than the required minimum (from two points to five), but the repeat business recovery numbers fell a bit short of the target (only 4.5 percent). Trey's management projects that as KM becomes an established part of the company's customer delivery system, repeat business will continue to increase as customer confidence grows.

This KM solution greatly increased the ability of Trey Research's employees to research and resolve customer and dealer inquiries, which resulted in increased revenue. Time and costs savings were also associated with the community site, where employees can more efficiently collaborate on documents. From chaos to a well-ordered collaborative process, the Trey Research example demonstrates the best of what KM has to offer in support of business objectives and goals.

Decisions About Content

An organization must make decisions on ownership, policies, standards, and practices that enable employees to easily identify content, ensure that it is used by those who most need it, and ensure that it is authoritative. These decisions are best tied in at natural points in the business process and made within those parts of the organization where the desired results are attainable. Common organizational decisions to consider are:

1. Agreement by key content providers on standards for knowledge capture.

2. Adoption by content managers of core vocabularies and clear ownership of the vocabularies.

3. Adoption of a taxonomy and agreement on visual mapping as defined in Chapter 6 and Chapter 10, "Knowledge Searching and Services."

4. Assignment of vocabulary and taxonomy management either to owners who agree to follow and coordinate common practices or to a central group with sole responsibility.

5. Agreement, accountability, and standards for content quality and availability by content owners and managers, including individual contributors.

6. Agreement on roles and responsibilities between those who own the information and knowledge and those who manage it, particularly

with respect to the change control process. (See the in-depth discussion of these points in Chapter 5.)

7. Definition of business requirements for organizing the information and knowledge, and communication of those requirements to the applications platform team(s).

8. Agreement on a search environment. (See Part III, "The Technology of Knowledge Management," for a discussion of tools.)

Summary

KAs are owned, shared, used, and reused depending on where they fall in the Personal, Community, Corporate, and Public Spaces of the Knowledge Cycle. The flow of knowledge moves information through the layers of knowledge development, content management, and knowledge exposure. Structuring and building a well-conceived knowledge index guides the company's collaborative site. Exposing KAs through a well-conceived KM environment will continuously inform, enlighten, and train all who visit the site and reuse the content.

Content is the known

Innovation springs from the known

The Technology of Knowledge Management

If the only tool you have is a hammer, you tend to see every problem as a nail.

Abraham Maslow (1908–1970), American psychologist

So far we have discussed the principles of value-based knowledge management (KM) and how it relates to an organization's environment and processes. Now it is time to talk about the tools that help you assemble a KM solution.

Technology plays a vital role in any KM solution. As Figure III-1 shows, it provides support for both the creation and reuse of knowledge assets (KAs). KM participants, whether creating or reusing KAs, must be able to search for information, access it, and provide feedback in a seamless, logical, and integrated manner. And the technology you choose must allow users to collect, publish, update, and remove content.

PART III

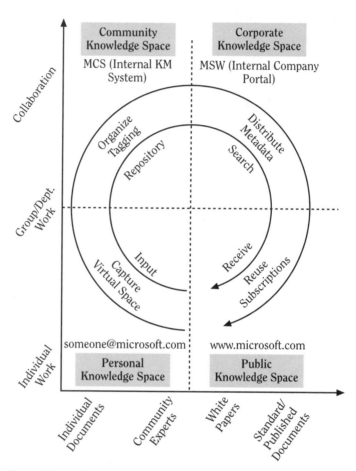

Figure III-1. *Knowledge Cycle—Technology Focus*

Until recently, KM took a back seat to other management efforts, such as quality or performance management. However, as connectivity has improved and the economic leverage of knowledge has become valued, we have seen an increase in interest as management turns its attention to the value created by knowledge workers. As a result of this change, the need for effective KM tools has become clear. Businesses are still feeling the pain of changing focus from managing tangible assets to understanding the nature of, and methods for, managing intangible assets. Crafting a solution that will provide the support for the content-management efforts as well as the collaboration needs of KM is the challenge for the information technology (IT) group. A wide range of personalization technologies, content management, and collaboration products can help you create sustainable KM services. However, although these technologies are available, most businesses are discovering that they must employ technologies that are integrated or compatible with their infrastructure and have a plan for scalability and growth to be truly effective. Microsoft offers such a solution through a combination of products. Integration from the desktop to the repository is required to make a solid KM environment.

Organization of This Section

In Part III we will address the key issues involving the technology solution, as well as ways in which Microsoft and Microsoft customers have solved this problem in their unique environments. We will highlight technology challenges and point to potential solutions for KM. Chapter 8, "Building a KM Foundation," focuses on the tools and technology that can help you create a KM system. In Chapter 9, "Measuring the Effectiveness of Your Repository," we discuss the reasons you should measure your repository's effectiveness and how you can do that. And in Chapter 10, "Knowledge Searching and Services," we highlight searching and other methods to connect your KAs to the people that need them.

Throughout Chapters 8, 9, and 10 we will reference the Microsoft Worldwide Consulting Services KM (MCS KM) system and its new prototype as a case study. This project was a bottom-up KM initiative started in the late 1990s. The program grew from a few hundred MCS field-based technology consultants sharing bits and pieces of implementation knowledge and documentation to over 3000 participants across MCS consulting and support personnel. The project collected nearly 9000 KAs, including project documents, code samples, and diagrams. As in most large organizations, some consulting practices were more committed to the KM concepts and invested time and resources in building the asset base. Other practices occasionally consumed KAs and provided assets on a sporadic basis. By and large, membership was voluntary, except in a few of the more KM dedicated practices, where consultants were required to belong to at least one technology community and submit the best of their work. In these practices consultants actually had KM objectives on their performance reviews each year. The project grew in popularity over two and a half years with sponsorship not only in many of the consulting practices worldwide but also in the product development groups. By 2001 it became obvious that if KM was going to become a major productivity tool for MCS, the program would need to evolve both from a technology perspective and an organizational sponsorship perspective. The original system, as you will see in the following chapters, was built on a Microsoft SQL Server 6.5 database joined to a Web front end. This system was upgraded as new versions of SQL Server and Web software were released. A new prototype system was built utilizing the latest Microsoft technology, including Microsoft SharePoint Portal Server, and presented to the consulting audience in July 2001. The majority of the screen shots in this book are from this prototype system. The MCS management elected to broaden and deepen the commitment to the collection and reuse of KAs not only by constructing a new system but also by reshaping the program from the top down. We are utilizing this program, as we did in Parts I and II, to demonstrate how a KM system could be constructed—not as a perfect example or the only right way to do KM. We strongly believe that KM is a continually evolving process within a company. Like knowledge itself, reinvention and rejuvenation are a natural fact of the KM life cycle—the MCS KM program is a successful living example of this reality.

Building a KM Foundation

The only irreplaceable capital an organization possesses is the knowledge and ability of its people. The productivity of that capital depends on how effectively people share their competence with those who can use it.

Andrew Carnegie (1835–1919)

A **knowledge management (KM) system** is the technology platform and infrastructure that an organization employs to share its knowledge. A successful KM system is one that is easily accessible by all knowledge workers in the organization. It should fit seamlessly into the users' current (or proposed) workflow processes, and it should be based on a sound understanding of the organization's culture and technology infrastructure. The knowledge assets (KAs) held by the system need to be readily accessible to the user at any time. The most important measure of success for a KM system is use. As we have established earlier, the return on investment (ROI) for KM is derived from the behaviors of the knowledge workers. The KM system's value comes from making those behaviors possible.

In this chapter we will discuss how the KM processes described in Part II, "The Process of Knowledge Management," work with tools and technology to complete the KM environment.

Technology's Role in a KM Solution

All KM solutions require some form of virtual environment, a library function, and processes to bind those two elements together. The KM technology you choose will play a critical role in each of these areas. Let's look more closely at these three main components:

- The virtual environment, or online community setting, gives knowledge workers, experts, and business leaders a way to share and communicate.

This environment tracks exchanges between community participants using electronic means, such as e-mail, discussion forums, or events. Any KM technology you choose should help employees connect and organize tacit knowledge development and exchange to solve problems that face their community.

- The library or repository function provides the foundation for finding, collecting, and reusing the explicit KAs already known, developed, or required by a company or community.

- Finally, processes tie together the virtual environment and the library function. Some of the processes—such as those that let you submit or find content in the system—are very closely tied to the technology solution, and they may change as technology changes. Other processes are bound to the organization's culture or vision of KM and are not as dependent on technology. Included in this category are reward and recognition programs (such as programs that award the type, amount, and method of content submissions), community leadership, and communications. There are also processes, such as the validation of KAs, that are tied both to the system (library) level and to the virtual (or community) environment.

Establishing KM in an organization requires careful attention to all three elements of the environment, as shown in Table 8-1.

Table 8-1.   KM Environment

The Virtual Environment	Connects people • Communication-centric • Tacit • Enabled by technology	Organizes information Examples: • Expert discussion on BizTalk • Transferring information on setting up security	Solves a problem Examples: • Brainstorming a solution to an indexing problem • Deciding how to sell KM to the automotive industry
		Processes	
The Library Function	Collects content • Document-centric • Explicit • Grounded in technology	Reuses content Examples: • Templates • Sample code	Finds content Examples: • Document on supply chain deployment in the retail sector • Notes on how to set up e-mail

Before we address the technology you could use to build a KM solution, let's take a quick look at the key strategy points from earlier chapters that directly affect your technology decision:

- **Get stakeholder sponsorship.** As discussed in Chapter 1, "Knowledge Is the Foundation of Business," Chapter 3, "Knowledge and the Business Culture," and Chapter 4, "An Implementation Framework," you need to ensure that key stakeholders are involved in the development, design, and implementation process from the beginning. This will help build a system in which the users feel ownership, and owners will put care into the design of a system because they will need to use it.

- **Plan to support measurement and reporting.** Remember that what is measured is managed. We discussed earlier the importance of linking KM to the basic productivity and accountability mechanisms within the organization. To support the KVA framework (see Chapter 2, "Placing a Value on Your Knowledge Management Investment") or any other designated metrics program, a KM system needs to capture and save information on content and usage.

- **Draw on past experience.** Learn from other projects that have been started in the organization or elsewhere. You can save time and effort by reusing or building on similar internal projects and industry examples, if they are available. Use these as a source of information about what has or has not worked for others.

- **Integrate with the way users work.** A successful system will allow users to continue to work efficiently. If possible, let the KM system be part of the organizational workflow rather than a demand for change. By developing integration points or links to existing applications that employees use, your company can fully make use of its KAs. This proactively provides users with information they need to do their jobs more efficiently. As users change the ways in which they work, the system must change with them.

- **Make it easy to use.** Limit the number of steps required for users at every stage. The fewer process steps, the less confused the participant will be, and the fewer technology components that will be required to support the actions. This type of planning will save time later in maintenance and training.

- **Keep it simple—especially in the beginning.** Take it one step at a time; you cannot build a successful complex system overnight. Do not try to deliver everything all at once. Determine the core elements of the project, deliver them, and measure success and user satisfaction before adding additional components.

- **Recognize the content life cycle.** In general, content is created, captured, organized, accessed, and used. In a well-designed solution, the technology should handle routine issues involving content management (such as author notification or archiving recommendations). By letting the technology solution handle these aspects of KM, the KM system can save valuable time and resources of both knowledge workers and content managers.

- **Plan for change!** To be successful, every system must evolve. System evolution requires good initial planning, scaleable architecture, and system documentation. Using good development practices will produce a solution that can change with the team's requirements. Keep your development team focused on the goal statement ("We need KM because…") and not on just building or buying a system. Do your planning, and make sure the proposed system will work in your environment. Get user and customer feedback early and often. If you are supporting a geographically dispersed population, you might need to consider a physically distributed system for access speed and local filtering of content submissions. This will keep the system aligned not only to your business goals but also to the way people work in your organization.

Planning Your KM Solution

The solution roadmap in Figure 8-1 provides an overview of the key project stages in a KM initiative. Of course, each organization will develop a unique project path, but these common stages should be evident in any good technology plan.

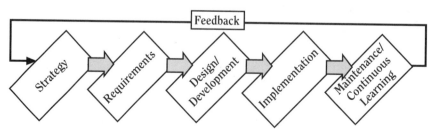

Figure 8-1.   *Solution Roadmap*

This five-stage project plan has been used in one form or another in most Information Systems texts for the last 20 years. Let's consider each of the phases with regard to a KM project:

1. **Strategy.** In this phase you define the context of KM for your organization, specifically the business and competitive strategies and the objectives and measures of success. This information guides the KM strategy throughout the project and ensures that the KM solution meets the business needs.

2. **Requirements.** In this phase you spell out all the requirements of the KM system—the environment (the content needed and the people involved), the process (who is involved, where it takes place, and the organizational support for KM), and the enabling technology. This stage includes an analysis of how ready the organization is to install a KM system and what the intended users want and need from the solution. It also includes determining what the actual knowledge needs are, including the type of knowledge needed, where it is located, and the best approaches for collecting and sharing that knowledge. (See the next section, "Strategy and Requirements Planning Stages," for a detailed discussion of this phase.) This is the time to gather baseline data on the current knowledge needs of the business (as described in Chapter 3) with regard to content and connectivity. You can then use this data to validate requirements during the design stage. And, finally, at this stage you determine the actual measures of success so that it is clear what is needed and how it should be measured going forward. The result of this stage is a comprehensive set of requirements that draw from best practices, user needs, and the unique culture of your business, and are tied to measures of accountability with your organization.

3. **Design and development.** In this phase you focus on designing and building the KM system using the requirements that your organization has outlined. This includes defining the KM technology-related processes and aligning them to the organizational processes defined in Chapters 3, 4, and 5, as well as selecting and building the technology solution.

4. **Implementation.** Now is the time to roll out the new KM system. Rolling out new KM technology and processes is a challenge that can be met if organizational implementation activities (such as ongoing communication, training on the KM system, and alignment of perfor-

mance measurements and rewards) are in place first. Implementation is, therefore, more than a go-live date; it includes all the work done to ready the organization, to roll out, and to monitor and adjust the processes and system to the organization in the real world.

5. **Maintenance and ongoing learning.** The last phase of the KM initiative is to sustain the new KM system, making sure it evolves as business and user needs change. People and processes will need to be in place to keep the system running on a daily basis. You will need to set up feedback channels so that new business goals, organizational changes, and user requirements are systematically collected and integrated into ongoing planning and releases. This ensures that the KM system is current, meets changing business demands, and improves based on lessons learned, evolving technologies, and best practices.

The rest of this chapter explains each of the five stages in some detail.

Strategy and Requirements Planning Stages

Two general approaches can be used in the first stages of a KM solution plan: top-down and bottom-up. A **top-down** approach typically starts high in the organization and looks at the big picture. Top-down planning generally involves the executive or senior level management of the entire organization or business unit. This type of planning generally links an overall KM strategy to the organizational goals. Top-down strategy tends to involve systematically developed plans, budgets, and organizational support for KM from the senior management level down through the entire organization. As described in Chapter 3, this type of planning starts with the organization's business strategy, objectives, and goals. The KM strategy is then built to support these business goals. In this approach, KM is seen as a core business strategy in and of itself, and KM planning and activities are closely integrated into other strategic initiatives, such as product development.

The top-down approach is best suited for large organizations that have strong executive support for and involvement with KM. The benefits of this approach are a close alignment of corporate strategy with departmental planning, and a clear link between business goals and the KM program. Drawbacks may include a significant commitment of time and resources for a large-scale project, an increased need for gaining and sustaining broad executive sponsorship, bottlenecks at the top, decision-making delays due to a corporate-wide hierarchy, and the risk that the effort will not connect with the needs of the grassroots (actual knowledge worker) user community.

A **bottom-up**, or grassroots, approach typically starts with a particular business problem, in a specific business unit, that can be addressed through KM. The focus is on using a KM program to address a specific problem or take advantage of a specific opportunity. It is often a pilot approach, which starts small, and has the goal of creating small successes and momentum that can later win executive sponsorship by demonstrating its value and, in time, serves as an example to other parts of the organization.

For grassroots efforts you can apply the same five-stage project approach shown earlier in Figure 8-1, with a narrower scope and smaller audience. The key difference is that the scope is at the business unit level, rather than the corporate level, and is much more tactical in nature. Leadership and sponsorship at the business unit level is required, and all the activities will tend to focus on tactical and local issues.

The bottom-up approach is best suited for organizations lacking strong executive understanding of and support for KM, and for cultures that are more entrepreneurial and decentralized in nature. Benefits of this approach are:

- Support and sponsorship at the local or front-line management level
- A KM solution that is truly built for the users, because they are initiating it
- The opportunity for small victories that can demonstrate value before considering expansion or application into other parts of the organization

Drawbacks may include:

- Difficulty getting the project off the ground (due to a lack of resources or funds)
- Potential overlap or lack of integration with other related initiatives
- Increased need for communication and evangelism once the solution is implemented
- Overreliance on technology, because it is often seen as a quick win and implemented first
- Risk of the effort being derailed due to competing efforts or projects the organization considers to be a higher priority

Regardless of the approach, you should consider and plan for the basic KM elements. You will need to integrate organization strategy, culture change, technology, and processes into the plan. Your plan should include a current state ("As Is") assessment, a future state ("To Be") definition, a gap analysis, an integrated process and system design, an implementation, and a maintenance plan. The key differences between the top-down and bottom-up approaches are in scope, level of sponsorship (corporate or business unit), and the breadth of the KM solution. Whether you institute a top-down or bottom-up approach, you and other KM leaders need to keep in mind a few key questions before launching the project:

- What is the problem or opportunity that could benefit from KM? What is the business case?

- What are the knowledge requirements? What knowledge is important to the users? What is the best way to capture, organize, and distribute knowledge for reuse?

- What process, technology, and organizational enablers are required for the KM solution to be accepted and successful?

- How will the KM solution be tracked and measured? How will benefits and ROI for KM be calculated? (See Chapter 2 for suggestions.)

- How will lessons and successes be documented and shared? How will knowledge be transferred to other parts of the organization?

Design/Development Stage

Once you have formulated a KM plan, and its related requirements, the project moves into the design and development stage. Although these are two distinct operations, they are tightly coupled and often appear to be one stage. In the discussion that follows we will single out some of major design and development issues that you, as a KM sponsor, should look for in the project plan.

Design the Structure and Process

An organization's KM structure and its KM process are two different things. The structure looks at how a KM system will be defined, built, implemented, and maintained. The process design looks at the specific ways of creating, capturing, organizing, and distributing the knowledge and, as discussed in Chapter 3, is

reflective of the organization's culture and the users' knowledge requirements. Chapters 5, 6, and 7 concentrated on the processes that will be needed
to achieve your goals. This chapter, along with Chapters 9 and 10, will concentrate on the structural design of the solution.

In general terms, you can look at a KM system's structural (or architectural) design as a three-tier model, with each tier performing specific functions and using different technologies. Figure 8-2 shows the basic three-tier
design:

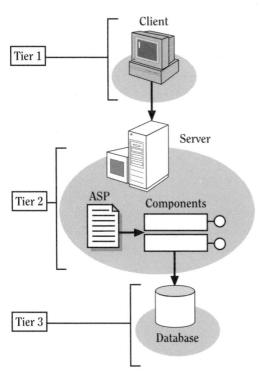

Figure 8-2.   *Three-Tier KM Architecture*

- Tier 1 represents the user interface (UI) and navigation methods and
  tools. This is where the entire user experience takes place. Not only
  does this layer provide a graphical interface so that users can interact
  with the application, input data, and view the results of requests, but
  it also manages data manipulation and formatting once the user (also
  known as the client computer) receives it. In Web applications, the
  browser performs the tier 1 tasks. Microsoft Internet Explorer and
  Digital Dashboard (explained later in this chapter) are examples of
  such an application at this level.

- Tier 2 methods and tools provide a link between the interface and data services layers. This tier contains the business logic established in the requirements analysis (performed during the planning stage). Business logic, which states the rules that govern application processing, connects the user at one end with the data at the other. The functions that the rules govern closely mimic everyday business tasks and can be a single task or a series of tasks. Applications at this level might include Microsoft Internet Information Server (IIS), Microsoft SharePoint Portal Server, and Microsoft Exchange 2000 Server.

- Tier 3 represents the data services, provided by a data store, which manage and provide access to the application data. Data stores can be structured (a structured query language [SQL] database, for example) or unstructured (like Exchange, or Microsoft Message Queuing). A single application may enlist the services of one or more data stores.

The first step in determining your development strategy is to recognize that there is a KM spectrum. On one end of the spectrum is a collaboration system, such as SharePoint Portal Server with its focus on workflow, shared document development, and chat rooms. On the other end are information portals designed to deliver corporate information, such as benefits plans and job postings, and receive limited data, such as address changes. At the onset, your development strategy should be based on the overall business or competitive strategy, the specific business problems or opportunities being targeted, and the type of knowledge that needs to be shared and used. Most often, the strategy is a combination, but with a stronger focus on one over the other (80/20). The direction and emphasis for your solution should have been clearly stated in the requirements gathering step in the planning stage.

Change Management Control and the Feedback Loop

Expect change as part of your project. No matter how well you define your requirements or plan your system, something will be missed or a requirement will change. Perhaps there is a law of nature that dictates a minimum set of these changes just to frustrate every project manager and software developer. Feedback at all stages of the project should be validated not only against design criteria but also against the KM strategy and business requirements. In today's fast-paced economy and business climate, you need to ensure that your KM solution stays in step with the evolution of your business. A well-established feedback loop is the most effective mechanism for accomplishing this task; an annual project review may often be too late to save the project from falling behind the needs of the business. Put checkpoints into the project review process to ensure that change control is part of the development and implementation stages of the plan. For example, you might find that a feature agreed to during the design phase (such as pop-up alerts on feedback forms) turns out to be disruptive during the testing phase.

Your development team will need to have a change control process in place to deal with these required changes as well as the innovative ideas that simply occur to people as the project unfolds. Without a good change control process, both situations can derail your project with unscheduled work and unplanned changes. Delivery delays, unless fully understood and agreed to, result in unhappy customers and cost overruns.

Scalability Considerations

With the increasing complexities of e-business and globalization, knowledge—and the management of knowledge—is becoming a strategic issue. As a company grows and its employees grow in number and become geographically dispersed, its KM solution will need to grow (or scale) as well. As these growth demands put pressure on the system, performance becomes a major issue. You may experience degradation in access time or search time as more users come online or seek access outside the main facility. You need to consider scalability early in the design process and carefully consider it from the environment (content and people), process, and technology perspectives. Do not let a simple or inexpensive solution constrain the spread of knowledge at a critical growth point in your company's future. Look forward and design for growth.

Development: Selecting Technology Components and Methods

All KM systems have at their heart a library or document-centric repository, as shown in Figure 8-3. The technology decisions around each of the numbered elements in Figure 8-3 will be discussed in the next few pages. Throughout this discussion we will reference the Microsoft Consulting Services (MCS) KM solution (described in the introduction to Part III) and the three-tier architectural model described earlier in this chapter to highlight how technology can enable an organization's KM decisions. The structure and products you use to achieve your KM solution will depend on the specific needs of your business. The following discussion highlights some of the Microsoft products that were used (or will be used) by MCS in the development of its KM solution. The goal of this discussion is to raise some technology points regarding how a KM solution could be developed from off-the-shelf components, not to provide an in-depth discussion of the products or technology. Additional technical discussion of these products can be found on *http://www.microsoft.com* or by contacting MCS.

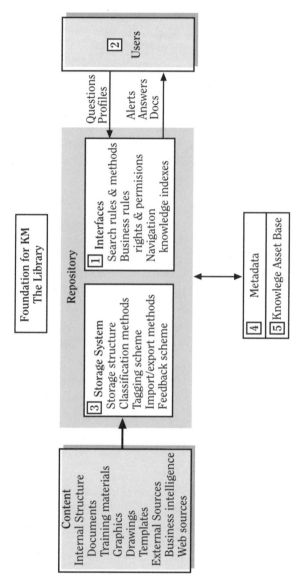

Figure 8-3.   *MCS KM Foundation (The Library)*

1. Interface Components

The suggested interfaces shown in Figure 8-3 represent a wide variety of options that knowledge workers can use to create, capture, organize, access, and use content. The most visible element of the KM architecture is the UI. The UI tools that users employ to manage access to services (such as community news or events) should allow a highly customizable workspace to accommodate different users' needs. Many people will want news items from specific communities, but not all communities, to appear routinely on their startup screen. Creating this system can be as easy as connecting some existing technologies, such as Microsoft Digital Dashboard, Microsoft Exchange 2000 Server, Microsoft SharePoint Portal Server technologies, and Microsoft Content Management Server (MSCMS), within your organization's current technology infrastructure. These products are examples of applications that provide user interfaces for KM systems while utilizing commands and tools that are familiar to users of Microsoft Office.

Microsoft's SQL Server Digital Dashboard 3.0 was used to form the front-end interface component of the MCS KM solution. Digital Dashboard, like similar Web interface tools, is a customizable solution that allows users to consolidate personal, community, corporate, and external information on one screen. This technique provides MCS KM users with single-click access to KA searching, collaborative tools, and metrics analysis. It provides an integrated view of diverse sources of knowledge so that field consultants can make better decisions. With this type of Web interface, every folder of information, private or public, can have a home page assigned to it. By attaching the desired home pages to their dashboard, users can create custom views by project, team, or organizational unit. With the **digital dashboard** approach, every user in the organization can have a centralized and customized information portal. If you host your data in Exchange 2000 Server public folders or in SQL data tables, users can selectively synchronize the data from the server and make it available offline. In this way, MCS used a digital dashboard to provide data access anytime, anywhere.

Another component incorporated into the MCS KM solution is Exchange 2000. Exchange, along with IIS (for Internet connectivity) and SQL Server (for data storage), provides many of the services for the tier 2 connectivity layer identified in Figure 8-2. Exchange 2000 Server provides an efficient way of creating, storing, and sharing information and provides a platform for collaboration and messaging that allows knowledge workers to access information in real time. Exchange 2000 Server also provides conferencing, instant messaging, and a unified platform for e-mail, voice mail, fax, and page messages that MCS uses extensively. Exchange 2000 Server is closely integrated with Microsoft Windows 2000 Active Directory service, providing MCS with a single point of management for the administrators and simplifying certain management, security, and distribution processes. It also allows users to announce their online presence, so users can see who is online and who is not. This feature is often used during community conference calls to ask questions of the speaker without interrupting the flow of the presentation.

A new technology that MCS is now integrating into its KM solution is SharePoint Portal Server. SharePoint Portal Server employs a standardized approach to integrating many of the tier 1 and tier 2 components that were previously used by MCS to develop its solution. For example, it uses a digital dashboard with new KM requirements for document sharing. SharePoint Portal Server, in addition to providing the digital dashboard technology, gives users the ability to share and publish information by using a search engine that is combined with data access and indexing services. This provides a single location to initiate searches for information stored in various places. SharePoint Portal Server also provides subscription features that allow a user to be notified in the portal or by e-mail. Searching is extensible to include custom content types.

You can use SharePoint Portal Server to categorize documents for better organization and layout. Features such as document versioning and check-in and check-out management allow you to implement a document workflow management system. SharePoint Portal Server provides tight integration with the Office XP suite of products and lets users manage their documents with familiar tools. SharePoint Portal Server also provides a portal with a customizable digital dashboard front end for optimum manageability.

A new addition to the KM environment is MSCMS—a new tool set to support the KM information distribution needs on the Web. This component allows companies to quickly develop and manage their portal solutions by providing in-context Web page authoring templates, real-time Web content updates, revision tracking, and page archiving. It implements a flexible workflow system that ensures that content is correctly approved before it goes live on the Web site. Content scheduling allows users (such as community leaders) to schedule Web page content and archival times. Because the content in MSCMS is segregated from the presentation template, the software allows dynamic template switching. In essence, your Web page layout can change in real time. These techniques keep content fresh for the user with minimal load on system administration. Web site publishing is often an administrative nightmare for the KM staff. Providing Web site management tools allows you to distribute to widely dispersed community leaders the responsibility for updating Web pages without extensive administrative support. Including

Web management tools in your KM solution will help not only to manage the site but also to keep your staffing requirements under control.

2. Common Desktop Tools Components (Users)

Tier 1 desktop tools (such as Office XP) are a great platform on which to build your custom interfaces. Using them means that users get to work with applications they are already familiar with, and that means less training. In addition, Microsoft desktop applications contain common development interfaces to facilitate connecting database and Web-based functions to your users. The MCS KM system receives KAs from the extended Microsoft Office family of applications, including Microsoft Word, Microsoft Outlook, Microsoft Excel, Microsoft PowerPoint, Microsoft Access, and Microsoft Project. This content is seamlessly received and maintained in the SQL Server database in its original format (such as .doc or .xls) for easy access by other users with the same desktop applications.

MCS KM was built on the feature sets of the Office applications by developing some simple Office add-in components (add-in code built by the MCS KM development team and linked to the standard Office products). These components allow users to submit content to the repository through any of the Office applications. Once this add-in component is installed, it becomes available to the user simply by clicking the File drop-down menu in any application. The installed add-in component appears along with the standard commands of Save, Save As, and Close, and provides the users with a link to Submit Content Form for the MCS KM system. Upon clicking this link, the MCS KM submission form opens, and users can send the content directly to the repository. This integration provides a method for submission that fits directly with the way MCS consultants work. Seamless integration with daily workflow makes technology a KM behavioral enabler, not a barrier.

3. Management Services Components (Storage Systems)

Technology management services, invisible to all users except the KM administrators, are used in larger KM applications. Most of these services are provided as part of the Microsoft .NET Server family. They help to simplify the implementation of content administration as well as to sort out many of the application-layer connectivity issues (providing the means to connect a variety of databases or Web servers). These services can include searching and publishing methods, collaboration tool connectivity, tracking and workflow mechanisms, versioning, replication, and backup of data. In more advanced systems these services support the delivery of content for offline viewing and updating.

4. Data Access Methods

Development and data access technologies are what bring these systems together. These elements of tier 3 connect the stored information to the services in tier 2 that the user accesses when requesting or submitting a KA. MCS used a variety of Microsoft data access and development tools to bring together its KM solution, such as Active Data Objects (ADO), that allowed for the integration of any type of content (code, Word documents, and so on). The development interfaces built into different applications can be accessed using Microsoft Visual Studio tools or scripting languages like VBScript and Active Server Pages (ASP). Developers use these tools to execute the commands issued by the tier 2 interfaces, which are in turn triggered by requests from the tier 1 desktop.

5. Data Storage Methods

Data stores, built in SQL Server 2000, are the core of the MCS KM repository. These are the tier 3 repositories where the KA content is stored. The type, source, and rules of KAs guide the formation of the KM storage system.

KA content is the wealth of information that organizations strive to manage and share with their employees, partners, customers, and the public. This content comes in all forms—documents, multimedia files, data, code, e-mail, and so on. It is important to understand what content means in the context of the technology proposed for your KM solution. The best solution may well be a combination of applications such as SharePoint Portal Server and MSCMS along with a SQL Server 2000 repository and Exchange 2000 Server.

SharePoint Portal Server and MSCMS define content differently and address different organizational issues. To SharePoint Portal Server, content is business information that is contained in document format or e-mail and made available through the SharePoint Portal, and is stored in a database. To MSCMS, content, as we discussed earlier, is defined as rich Web content, including text, graphics, video, and documents. Business users publish this Web content using templates on Internet, intranet, and extranet sites built with MSCMS.

Content can be stored and accessed through a variety of tools, depending on the ultimate use of the information. The Exchange 2000 Server Web Store, for example, is a storage technology for unstructured content like documents and Web pages or for messaging content like e-mail messages, tasks, and calendar entries. SQL Server 2000 and Access are better suited for storing structured content (associated with a structured taxonomy or knowledge index). In the MCS KM group, the decision was made to use SQL Server 2000 and Windows 2000 Server file share storage to provide better data measurement from analytical services.

The specific technology components your team will use to build your KM solution will be dictated by your current or planned infrastructure, the type of knowledge you will be storing, and the communication needs of your users. Collocated users have higher bandwidth and greater connectivity than geographically dispersed users. For global companies, local requirements and bandwidth issues may require a distributed model.

Implementation Stage

To implement a collaborative KM environment (as described in Chapter 4 and Chapter 5), you need to support a great deal of tacit-to-tacit and tacit-to-explicit knowledge exchange and conversion. As shown in Figure 8-4, in collaborative environments, knowledge exchange occurs by means of e-mail and other online mediums outside of the library or document-centric system components. This environment represents more than just the communities of practice described in Chapter 5. As part of this service, the technology must support the user interface, participant-community communications (peer-to-peer, peer-to-community, and leader-to-participant), connectivity to the library, personalization (an evolving concept), and customer and business intelligence information. Often this connectivity can involve outside partners, the Internet, or intergroup links (dynamic or static in nature). Finding expertise (both static, in the library, and dynamic, in a live person) is part of the virtual space that the technology will need to address in a truly collaborative environment.

Persistent conversations carried on electronically over the Internet and intranet and through other forms of messaging become a focal point for the virtual space in the KM system. Because collaborative KM tries to make it easier for an organization's people to create new knowledge and innovate, the technology needs to provide an environment that supports knowledge sharing and manages the peer-to-peer and peer-to-expert exchanges in an organization. Most of this information exchange occurs through e-mail in what are often referred to as "threaded conversations." A threaded conversation is a collection of e-mail messages that reference each other. The threads form a "tree," with the initial message being the start of the tree and each reply forming a branch on the tree. Knowledge workers are faced with two challenges: first, how to sift through the sheer volume of information, and second, how to determine the credibility of any respondent. Over time and with some effort, community members develop individual senses (or a feeling about the credibility) about who the real experts are within a community. This takes time, and the information is not transferable to other people. Because of these challenges, effective KM in this part of the environment requires a new set of tools.

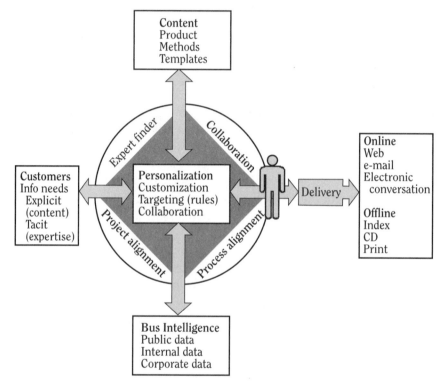

Figure 8-4.   *The Virtual Space*

Discovering experts in electronic communication, such as e-mail threads, is slowly becoming a reality. Microsoft Research developed a set of tools, called Netscan, for illustrating the structure of discussion threads like those found in USENET newsgroups and the patterns of participation within these discussions.[1] A sample of the reports a user can view online from Netscan is shown in Figure 8-5. The reports visually demonstrate to the participant the depth of a particular conversation, who is answering, and how many subthreads spun off the conversation. An important feature of this reporting tool is the author detail report. In this report, a knowledge consumer (someone seeking an

---

1. M.A. Smith and A.T. Fiore. "Visualization Components for Persistent Conversations." *Proceedings of ACM Computer-Human Interaction 2001.*

answer) can quickly look at the history of a given author (the respondent to the question) to find out if that author has given correct answers to others (and how often) and even to see previous answers to assess their quality. The goal of this type of expert finder is to allow the knowledge consumer to develop a sense of confidence in the knowledge provider that is often missing in the virtual world.

Microsoft Research created Netscan to give the more than 91,000 users of its large newsgroups a tool to make value-based decisions that are to some extent based on the information they received in these communities. Data mining the messages in these newsgroups generated the data used in the Netscan project. From this data—messages and the patterns of replies in threads—the user may infer certain characteristics, such as the importance of a message within a thread or the role of a respondent in an online group, as shown in Figure 8-5. As you can see in the sample report from the Netscan Web site, a list of posters (people asking and responding to questions) is shown both as a composite report card on the community and in an Author Tracker report. The Community Report Card gives the viewer an overall picture of community-based conversations, whereas the Author Tracker breaks the specific conversations down to tell you the number of postings made by the contributor. Also, the interpersonal connection component of the reporting tool displays what is called a "sociogram," a feature that relates users with those they reply to and who reply to them (by thread, respondent, or subject). People viewing these reports can immediately see what type of content a particular author feels confident to respond to as well as how many responses he or she has given, and how many postings are questions and how many are answers. These characteristics, along with the others shown on the public Netscan Web site (*http://netscan.research.microsoft.com*), allow the system to begin building respondent credibility ratings automatically. As these credibility ratings build, there is less need for the types of rating systems, or feedback scores, used by Web sites like Amazon.com, the online bookstore, and eBay, the auction Web site. Though progress is being made in building tools (like Netscan) that make electronic conversation threads easy to navigate, surveying users is still useful. Invasive methods of soliciting feedback on the information and data presented by the KM system may take time from work, but still offer a highly valuable format for gathering feedback on authors, experts, and information.[2] When you combine such feedback with the measures derived from the message data itself in order to generate detailed histories and reputation scores, you get greater accuracy than you can get with message data alone. Microsoft Research is currently investigating unobtrusive ways to include this functionality in future versions of office productivity software and internal KM systems.

---

2. *Ibid.*

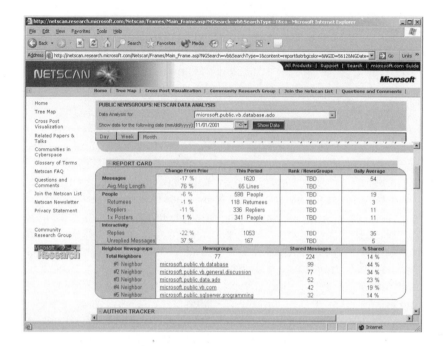

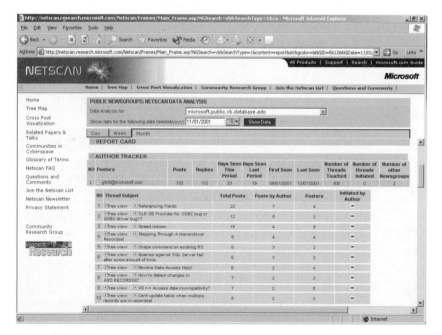

Figure 8-5. *Netscan Reports*

The tools and approaches presented support a KM system infrastructure that provides the organization with:

- Increased organizational effectiveness by creating the ability to find the information and expertise that the participants need, when they need it, fast—regardless of where they are

- A common framework that facilitates the easy sharing of experiences and best practices

- A means to facilitate work across organizational and geographical barriers through "global" communities

Maintenance Stage

To ensure that your KM system continues to deliver value, you need to maintain and protect that value. These efforts include regular hardware and software maintenance, disaster planning, security audits, and application updates. How you maintain your hardware and system software platform (operating system) depends on the guidelines from your organization's information technology (IT) department. Maintaining the platform will help ensure system reliability and performance. Do not forget to plan for disasters. Make sure you have a disaster recovery plan and, more importantly, that you have tested it.

Because the system used by MCS is an intranet-based application, the Microsoft corporate network security protects against outside intrusion. Internally, the system is available to workers and relies on Windows 2000 authentication to identify who is accessing the system. Through click tracking and change tracking, Microsoft can audit who is using the system and what they are doing. MCS system uses a three-tier security structure.

- **First level.**   All workers can submit and utilize content.

- **Second level.**   A smaller group of identified key users can edit and review content submitted to the repository.

- **Third level.**   An even smaller group has full access to maintain the site content and dashboard layout.

Because KM is a continuous learning engine for the organization, the KM system should also be a continuously evolving system. Your system needs to grow and evolve as your needs change and organization grows. You should provide a mechanism for users to provide feedback directly. Usage analysis will help you determine what is being used and what is not, and enable you to plan changes based on actual usage.

Technology changes rapidly, and the way people work and exchange information and ideas can change rapidly too. To keep up with the change, your system needs a feedback loop and must be responsive to change.

Summary

Your choice of technology depends on the goals and infrastructure available to build the solution. You can organize a combination of applications and components to fill nearly any need a company has defined for KM to fill. This can range from a system that is used simply to publish company-wide information to a fully collaborative environment. Once KM goals are established, the team chosen to design the solution needs to review the features and technology requirements of the currently available technology to determine the best fit. As with any major technology implementation, a KM solution needs to be planned, designed, developed to the design, and, finally, implemented and maintained. Many of these functions require not only maintenance but also regular updating. Planning, building, and implementing a technology solution is only the beginning—both the solution and the enabling technology will need to be continuously reviewed in light of changes in the business and the changes in technology.

Strategy drives processes

Components support functionality

Measuring the Effectiveness of Your Repository

*My experience of the world is that things left to themselves
don't get right.*

Thomas Henry Huxley (1825–1895), English biologist[1]

As we saw in Chapter 8, "Building a KM Foundation," a knowledge management (KM) system's repository is one of its key components. This library-like function gives a structure to the knowledge assets (KAs) and gives all users access to the explicit organizational knowledge they need. The repository is the electronic equivalent of the bricks-and-mortar library found in most cities. Just as these libraries do with their books and other materials in a library, an electronic repository provides methods for storing, managing, and measuring the use of the KAs contained in it. Today the KM-enabling technology has evolved to a point where you can set up a basic repository quickly and easily. But before you give your software designers and developers that job, you need to take the time to consider what the repository will store and how you will monitor the use of the stored KAs. As we discussed in Chapter 8, these organizational goal statements shape the technology decisions you will make for your KM system.

The repository is at the core of the KM solution. It is the place KAs flow into and out of. It is critical to measure that flow, to determine not only the repository's vitality and growth, but also the use and reuse of its assets. In this chapter we will review some of the key technology issues concerning how you measure KM in your repository.

---

1. *Aphorisms and Reflections*, from the works of T. H. Huxley, selected by Henrietta A. Huxley. (London: Macmillan and Co., Ltd., 1907).

Measurement in Your KM System

As we saw in Chapter 2, "Placing a Value on Your Knowledge Management Investment," you need a way to tie KM to your employee and business review process and measure its impact. To accomplish this task, you will need to capture the data not just about your KM system operations but also about the KM behaviors of the participants—that is, the data that makes a KM value analysis possible. In Chapter 2 we introduced the KM Value Assessment (KVA) framework, which is a method of assessing the value that KM brings. Let's take another look at that framework in Figure 9-1. To help an organization meet its strategic goals, managers need performance baselines and tactical (in-process) measures from the KM system itself. A performance baseline is generated or established the first time an organization completes a KVA using the KVA framework methodology. The KM system should allow managers to view the in-process, or monthly, KM-related activity and behavior reports as tactical measures to guide their teams on a daily or routine basis. The quarterly, or routine, KVA framework reports tie knowledge workers' activities (things they are assigned to do, like writing a white paper), behaviors (how they perform the activities assigned, such as using templates or calling up existing KAs before starting a job), and performance goals (performance targets linked to company strategic goals) in one view or value chain. The results of a KVA analysis allow a business to determine the impact of a given value chain (a combination of work activities and behaviors) on profitability or production.

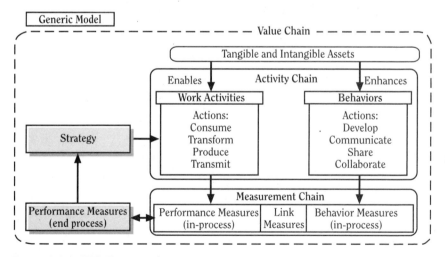

Figure 9-1. *KVA Framework*

A KM system should give you the measurements you need to check the health and vitality of your repository as well as the reuse of the KAs in it. Thus it is important to take some time to investigate *what* to measure before you develop and implement your KM system. KM metrics can be grouped into the following three general categories:

- **KM activities and behaviors.**   These in-process measures (current activity/behavior reports) track both the activities (actual work items) and the work behaviors (ways of completing assignments) of the participants, such as the number of visits to a Web site or the use of KAs such as code samples.

- **KM value correlations.**   These are the end-process measures (the correlated results) that relate individual and group activities and behaviors to the targets set for KM. These measures are most often developed as correlations to financial or production data reported by the standard accounting processes within a company. In the example used in Chapter 2, we looked at a consulting company that was seeking to improve its margin by 10 percent. If you follow the KVA model, you would identify consultants who completed projects on or above the specified margin levels first. Next, you would correlate these results to the KM behaviors performed by these same high performing consultants to develop a recommended baseline set of KM behaviors for a specified type of project activity (such as using templates when generating project proposals if the majority of successful projects utilized this technique). Historical trends will build a solid set of relationships between financial performance and KM behaviors. Over time, as data and confidence build, managers will become proficient at using this information to shape employee work behaviors in a proactive and constructive manner.

- **Management of the KM system and repository.**   System data (response time, availability data, and so on) and repository statistics (number of KAs, validations, and so on) are in-process measures of the KM system usage. Although these are important statistics about the KM project, don't confuse them with the statistics you get from activities and behaviors or KM value correlations, as explained above.

See Also   Chapter 2 has more information on the Knowledge Value Assessment framework and associated methodology.

> **Tip**   Do not forget to create rewards and recognition programs, as discussed in Chapter 5, "Creating and Sustaining Communities of Practice," to reflect achievements targeted by the KM project, KM performance, and strategic goal targets. As part of the business requirements for the system, metrics should be designed and set up to make these programs easy to administer, modify, and track.

The KM developers should place triggers (which are like electronic bookmarks or tags) in the KM system to capture and store the data on participant behaviors and activities. As part of the organizational and business analysis discussed in Chapter 3, "Knowledge and the Business Culture," and Chapter 4, "An Implementation Framework," the management team should have identified the major activities and related behaviors they expect as part of the business cycle. The software developers will need to set up measurement techniques (to accumulate totals against the various behaviors, such as template use or number of searches performed by a user). The KM tools should allow managers to use these measurements as group or individual snapshots or trends on a routine (daily, quarterly, annually) basis to guide knowledge workers. Managers can track financial or productivity figures in the accounting system for specific groups or individuals. If the numbers do not look positive, the manager could review the KM behaviors of the team or individual and, based on past correlations, recommend changes in the way the group or individual performs the activities. Routine correlations of KM behaviors to actual business results should be run and compared to the baseline value chain to ensure that managers are recommending the best work behaviors for the current business and economic environment.

As discussed in Part II, "The Process of Knowledge Management," an organization can track many KM behaviors and activities. We will first define behaviors and activities from a system perspective and then discuss how a KM system can track them.

KM Behaviors and Activities

Each organization must define the KM activities and behaviors that are important to its business. It is also important to define the time span over which you will track and present such data. When you introduce any new system or process, there will be a ramp-up or transition period, so it is important to measure and track changes during that time. The system administrator should set up measurements to track a wide variety of activities and behaviors identified as important to the business. In the next few pages we briefly discuss tracking Web activities and behaviors of participants in the virtual space, including:

- **Web site visits.**   The activity is visiting the site, but the behavior is reading specific items.

- **KA exchange tracking.**   The activity is KA use. One of the behaviors around this activity is recording if individual users are knowledge consumers or knowledge producers.

- **Knowledge-seeking activities.**   The activity is obviously seeking or searching. One of the many behaviors associated with it is what the user elects to do with the results.

- **Using Web-based content.**   If Web information, such as trends, new features, or competitive market data, supports activities that participants are asked to carry out (such as consultants or sales people writing competitive analysis reports), the leaders will most likely want to track the behaviors—in this case, viewing or downloading the information.

- **Persistent conversations (tacit conversations in the electronic space).** Participating in the conversation is an activity, but tracking who answered and who asked is one set of interesting behavioral measures.

Once management determines which activities and behaviors are critical to measure, the system developers will need to determine how to track them. It is preferable to have the tracking process designed into the system and not added as an afterthought, so it should be a key requirement in the design and development phase of the KM system.

Let's take the KM system used by Microsoft's Consulting Services (MCS) organization, described in the introduction to Part III, "The Technology of Knowledge Management," as an example. The system was designed to capture and record key activity and behavior patterns of the consultants participating in or using the system. This data is then stored in a back-end structured query language (SQL) database for later analysis. Two key activities and behaviors combinations captured included Web site usage and exchange of KAs. Let's look at both in more detail to see how these might be tracked in your organization.

Tracking Web Site Usage

One primary metric that participants in the MCS KM environment can see is **Web site visits**—who is using the KM system—by visiting the Web-based home, or primary, page. This is a KM activity (not usage), but it shows who has or has not taken that first step toward community interaction and participation. As Figure 9-2 shows, the home page log tracks which participants are using the Web-based components (such as events calendars or product news items) and how frequently the user goes to the home page. This log does not track what they are doing with the information. Subsequent logs (on other pages) or systems track user activities at a lower level. Event registration, for example, is recorded in a registration log by the learning group, and KA downloads or searches are recorded in its own logs. Home page visits is a key area to track during the initial deployment because it is an indicator of adoption—that is, how well the organization is accepting the KM system as a home base for KM activities. The MCS group wanted to find out the number of unique users, people visiting the site at least once per month, and the number of days between site visits per user. The unique visitors-per-month is a measure of breadth of adoption within the organization, and the days between visits provided a measure of the degree of adoption. To track this activity, the MCS team used the digital dashboard Web logs in the back-end Microsoft SQL Server 2000 database to record user and date-time information each time the home page was displayed.

Figure 9-2.   *Activity Counter*

Figure 9-2 shows a digital dashboard Web component used in the MCS KM system for displaying real-time, personal, and organization-wide usage information. The counter displays a rolling 30-day activity report highlighting individual visits, overall community visits, and KA reuse counts, as well as top submitters and community experts. Participants have reported that the information they get on KA submissions and reuse helps them find out who the "go-to" person in the community is when it comes to specific topics. The person submitting the most work in an area demonstrates confidence in his or her skills in that area. If a person's work is often reused by others, the user demonstrates coworker confidence in the author. The information displayed in MCS's Community Counter has been stored in the back-end database. Your KM developers can tailor a display like this to highlight what is important to your organization.

To align KM data by organizational group, the KM developers will need to make sure the KM system is linked to a human resources (HR) system so that you can obtain the organization/reporting structure information. This intersystem link is key to providing the right report to each group. This information allows a manager to determine which people or groups are, or are not, using the KM services. The KM leader or sponsor can then focus on learning why various groups are not engaged and work with them toward adoption. Reasons for low use might be related to connectivity, language barriers, or other business or cultural issues that did not surface during the planning stage. You can also use rewards and recognition programs, as discussed in Chapter 5 and Chapter 7, "Capturing Your Organization's Knowledge Assets," to promote or acknowledge groups with high participation rates.

Tip Watch for unexpected users of the system. They may point out other KM opportunities. For example, although the MCS KM system was designed and built to meet the needs of the MCS field consultant, it turned out to benefit all field-based support personnel, not just the consultants.

Another metric to seek is component usage. This is the statistic that tracks what users are doing when they get to the site. If your KM system provides more than just check-in/check-out/search functionality, you will want to track what parts are being utilized and by whom. Collaborative systems offer participants more than just a repository. Microsoft's MCS system, for example, includes components for Hot Topics, an Events Calendar, and links to other useful intranet sites, to list a few. (See Figure 9-3.)

To obtain this level of detail, the MCS development team created an ActiveX component to handle user click tracking; the clicks are recorded in a SQL Server 2000 database. By tracking and analyzing how people use the site, MCS is able to determine the type of product and service-specific information that consultants consistently seek. This knowledge then guides MCS efforts in locating highly valued information.

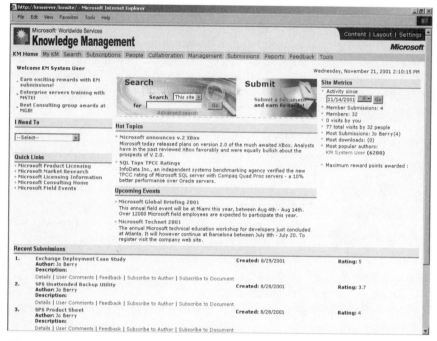

Figure 9-3.   *MCS KM System Technical Community Home Page*

Tracking Exchange of Knowledge Assets

In addition to site and component usage, KM leaders will want to track what participants give back to the system, or the **content submissions**. This is the production side of the KM equation and is also closely tied to the repository function. Measuring submissions gauges your inventory's size and growth. This is very important to track, but do not let this metric mislead you. Each organization must determine what growth rate and quality level is important to it. In general, during the initial deployment, most organizations will want to see this number growing or having a high (time-based) growth rate. Early in the KM program's life, it is important to show usage, excitement, and support, so having a growing asset base is important. But at some point each organization must shift from a "bulk is great" mentality to an emphasis on quality and value; at that point, the importance of measuring growth declines. The type, value, and frequency of submissions are behavior patterns that can be correlated to financial value statements, as discussed in Chapter 2. Submissions linked to key initiatives or product sales may also provide important input to valuation statements.

Any system should be able to track content submissions. For the MCS system, in our example above, a Web-based submission protocol to upload client-submitted documents was built. As part of the submission process, metadata (data tags used by the system to easily identify the contents of the submission once it has been stored) is captured and stored in a SQL Server 2000 database.

For reporting purposes, again a KM system should tie back to other systems within your organization, such as the HR system, to support organizational and work group performance analysis. As part of a rewards and recognition program, you need to identify groups and individuals who show the desired KM behaviors. Nearly as important is the ability to identify groups or areas that are not participating so that you can take corrective action. If you subscribe to the traditional 80/20 rule, 80 percent of your production most likely will come from 20 percent of your user population. Track it and see if you have the same producers month after month. Maintaining the right mix of knowledge producers and knowledge consumers is an important goal for KM leaders.

Because one of the main purposes of a KM system is reuse of KAs, you will naturally want to gauge **content downloads**, too. This is the consumption side of the KM equation. Without consumption, you have no value. The same points apply to analyzing reuse as for content submission. Reuse tracking tells who is using the content (and who is not), but also what content is being used. Content reuse is an important KM activity and behavior. It shows a shift in culture (employees who don't have to reinvent the wheel) and helps identify submitters of valued content. Again, to perform this type of reporting and analysis, you need to link to another system, such as HR. As described in Chapter 8, this should be a basic (tier 2) functionality of any KM system. Linking downloads to actual *reuse* of content is difficult but rewarding. Rewarding feedback that provides this information will help you develop needed data points for analysis. Some reuse data can be collected through noninvasive programmatic feedback forms, but true reuse data will come from qualitative survey studies. Reuse studies should be done quarterly or semiannually to ensure that system value is being realized. (A more detailed discussion on this technique can be found later in this chapter in the section entitled "Correlation Analysis.") Aligning KA acquisition by participants with new products and services (innovation), sales, or deliverables (such as service repairs or new code to clients) provides data for value-based reporting as well. In a study of the MCS KM repository in 2000, MCS determined that the repository lacked the content to support a new service that it was about to launch. As a result, community leaders are now seeking new assets to support the MCS consultants in the implementation of the new service. Once these assets are submitted or linked to the KM repository, MCS's goal will be to track their usage.

If your KM system uses a **layered repository** (that is, it contains KAs at various levels of validation, as described in Chapter 7) with different types or qualities of KAs, you will need to be able to report trends and analyze content submission and reuse according to these categories. All measures should be reported on a time basis (period by period or change per period) and reported as trends, rather than given as simple running totals. Track the trends, as these are indicators of changes in behavior and KM adoption.

The following two figures are examples of how the metrics tracked by the KM system can be displayed. Both Figure 9-4 and Figure 9-5 are reports that show changes in KM behavior over time and across six different technology-based virtual communities. Figure 9-4 and Figure 9-5 show similar participation and submission patterns by each of the communities measured. Correlating these results with other metrics within the company could inform the community leadership about behavioral drivers, such as marketplace shifts, product releases, or other company-specific events that drive KM participation.

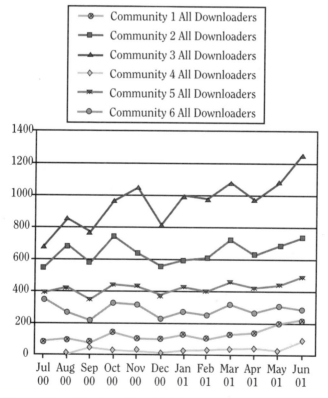

Figure 9-4. *Month-to-Month Distinct Consumers of Content by Virtual Community*

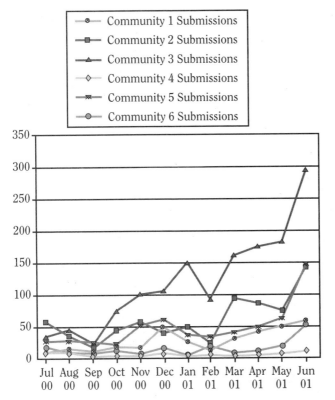

Figure 9-5.   *Month-to-Month Knowledge Asset Submissions by Virtual Community*

Tracking Knowledge-Seeking Activity

Knowledge workers need to connect not only with static KAs (as described in the earlier section of this chapter entitled "Tracking Exchange of Knowledge Assets") but also to other knowledge workers. Activities that occur around this tacit, or dynamic, knowledge connection are important indicators of a healthy knowledge-based environment. The tacit-to-explicit and tacit-to-tacit knowledge exchange information found in such activities as KA reuse and electronic (persistent) conversations help evaluate a community's strength and direction.

A great way to determine what employees want or need is to track and analyze what they are actually *searching* for. Successful **search results**, when combined with information about whether the results were downloaded, are useful to look at. This combination of KM behaviors is useful to include in your value analysis because it is another indication that the repository has the assets that consumers are looking for as well as using. To support this analysis, the search engine must support some type of logging (storing the search and result set metadata).

More important is analyzing search requests where no KAs are returned or, if returned, not downloaded. When no results are returned, that might be an indication that the repository is missing useful content and or that existing content might not be accurately tagged. If searching does return results, but they are not downloaded, what does that mean? Further analysis may indicate low-quality content or incorrectly tagged content (after reading the abstract, users might decide that this is not what they need) or that the consumer has insufficient bandwidth to download a large result set.

Persistent conversations, also called threaded conversions, which are performed by participants as part of online conversations, are also worthy of evaluation. (They are called "persistent" because they can be carried on over days or months by many people.) Often these conversations (or contextual collaborations) take on a life of their own, with many people participating, adding comments, and making suggestions. Persistent conversations can be conducted in chat rooms associated with the Web site, through e-mail, or by means of other messaging systems. As your collaborative KM system matures, being able to derive information on behavioral trends can help you develop a solid basis for identifying expertise and defining community issues. Current industry estimates show that knowledge workers spend at least one hour a day managing e-mail and that nearly half of all corporate knowledge is passed directly or indirectly though e-mail.[2] Participants ask questions of peers and subject matter experts in this space. The members of a community of practice can build community loyalty by quickly answering the questions and delivering the information. By monitoring threaded conversations, community leaders can determine who answers the questions. This expertise identification can not only lead to the identification of knowledge resources within the community, but also provide justification for community-based rewards and recognition programs. Building methods for tracking and analyzing persistent conversations has many KM rewards.

See Also   Additional information on using persistent conversations to analyze participation can be found in Chapter 2, and, to find expertise within CoPs, in Chapter 8.

---

2. Matt Cain. "Web & Collaboration Strategies." Meta Group. (March 23, 2001).

Tools such as Microsoft's Netscan technology collect, store, and map keyword clusters found in messages to a taxonomy (as described in Chapter 6, "Building Taxonomies") and then correlate these topics to the author. This process allows you to build a profile of authors and conversations that you can analyze. Analysis reports, such as an author profile, produced by the KM system and posted on the Web site, help to build user trust in answers provided by community members and are a good tool for managers to discover who in their group of employees or peers has expertise in a given subject.

KM Financial Value Analysis

Now that we have looked at some typical activity and behavior patterns the KM system could track, let's shift gears and summarize how this contributes to the bottom line or company value. This picture will vary by business, but one contribution that will likely be common to all businesses is the ability to increase productivity and efficiency through the intelligent application of KM behaviors and the availability of KAs. Saving time due to reuse (downloading) can translate into many different areas, such as:

- Increased efficiency (a faster turnaround on requests)

- Increased output (the ability to respond to more customers)

- Reduced risk (the feeling that "we have done this before, so I know how to do it")

- Increased resource utilization (the knowledge that "because we have done this before, I can use a less experienced resource")

Feedback Supports Analysis

In order for you to perform this analysis, the KM system must provide a feedback mechanism. As consumers use KM assets, the system must poll these users for their feedback so that you can capture and track information such as "how useful was this asset?" and "how much time did it save?" It is important that the system collect this feedback sooner rather than later because as the length of time increases between usage and feedback, the validity of the feedback declines. The process of capturing this feedback must be quick and easy so that consumers are inclined to provide it. The feedback process is also an important KM behavior that you need to monitor and reward.

You can use this rating/valuation process in addition to financial analysis to make it easier to discover valuable content and reward producers of valuable content. **Content management (CM)** can also use it as a flagging method for weeding out marginal content. As the system uncovers highly valued content (based on consumer ratings), that content can be bubbled up to the top of search results or rankings, highlighted on a "top 10 asset"-type list, and programmatically "pushed" to subscribers who have indicated in their personal profile that they want to receive high-valued content on a specific topic. You can reward producers of high-valued content in many ways, from having their content and name appear on the "top 10" list to receiving other awards at review time. By tracking the ratings, you have a systematic method for flagging content that needs to be removed (content with low value or low usage) or evaluated for improvement (content that is not deep enough or inaccurate).

The KM system used by MCS incorporates all of these feedback mechanisms. Microsoft experimented with different methods and times for when and how they collect user/content feedback. The primary lesson learned with regard to feedback was to focus on making the feedback/rating process simple and efficient and to make sure the user was asked questions specific to the value the analyst is trying to measure. MCS currently uses the results of the rating feedback (combined with reuse information) to flag content that needs to be retired or modified/enhanced.

Correlation Analysis

Feedback, as with any data set, has little value if it is not used to benefit or evaluate the process. Above all else, the ultimate goal is to provide a set of practical, tested, and reliable tools and ideas for the managers and knowledge workers to use in evaluating the business operation. Thus, completing the KVA by correlating the KM activities and behaviors to the target goals should be a critical final output of the KM reporting system. As we stated earlier, completing the value chain evolution gives managers and users information on the health and vitality of the communities, the KAs, and the effect of the KM practices on the business. (See Chapter 2 for a complete discussion of this topic.)

If the KVA model is not built into the system, you will need to extract the data from the KM system and other sources into a spreadsheet or database to build your correlation. This takes more time but can achieve the same result. This was the case with the original MCS KM system we discussed earlier, so a survey was conducted after two years of operation to gather the missing data. This data was collected from field consultants who were the heaviest consumers of content (that is, the people who downloaded the most KAs). The survey's primary objective was to generate more detailed data on reuse value. The feedback process did not require specific information on content use, but only requested a score for the item (*excellent, good, average, below average,* or *poor*). Thirty participants were selected, and Microsoft provided them with a list of content they had downloaded during a recent 30-day period and asked them to provide detailed feedback on how they used the content and how much value, in terms of time saved, they got from the content. Of the 30 participants, the MCS KM team received sufficient responses from 23. From this data, the MCS KM team was able to build a prototype valuation model that can estimate the value of a download. It is important to note that download does not necessarily mean reuse. Consultants in this environment often downloaded a set of KAs and then reviewed them offline to see which ones they use on their current assignment. This analysis allowed MCS to develop an approximate "discard rate" (the percentage of downloaded content that turned out to be inapplicable to the problem or question) that could be applied to the straight numeric download total to arrive at what the MCS KM team termed a "valued download" (downloaded content that was applicable to the problem or question). Based on a simple analysis, a time-savings estimate was developed for a valued download.

This was MCS's first attempt at this type of analysis on the KM usage data, and it validated that KM provides value to its organization. MCS will continue to perform a periodic, in-depth usage/value survey and refine its valuation model.

KM System and Repository Measures

How well the KM system (the application and the associated technology) is operating is very important to the KM project's success. If the technology does not offer a consistent, easy-to-use, and stable environment, you will lose your audience's attention. And that would, of course, harm your financial benefits. Thus, measuring KM system indicators such as site availability (is the site always available, does functionality correspond to the level of equipment and connection speed available to the average user, and so on) is extremely important for all business support systems. Monitoring availability is not necessarily a component of a KM system, but it is a service that must be available to all production systems. The important thing is that you define what availability means to your organization and establish availability targets (perhaps "24/7" system availability). These targets greatly depend on the type and nature of your business environment. If, for example, you have global users, your KM system needs to be available 24 hours a day. Or if you have field-based workers who connect only through a voice grade phone line, you will need compressed downloads. Once you have set the targets, make sure your operations and support teams can monitor and track them. Ensure that your contingency planning supports your goals.

Now that we have identified and discussed several of the metrics that might be tracked and have ensured that the KM system captures them, how is the data going to be made visible—that is, how can you show that information in reports? Again, this is going to vary by organization, but you will need to have a group of standard activity/value reports by time period plus an ad hoc reporting capability.

The MCS KM system relies on several canned (or standardized) reports and uses Microsoft SQL Server 2000 Analysis Services including online analytical processing (OLAP) and data mining for flexible data analysis. The canned reports represent the group's key performance indicators (its health metrics), displaying key KM activities by time period with trending over time. The OLAP cubes provide drill-down reporting that allows managers to see KM activities and behaviors for an entire group (summary level) as well as for individual participants.

Tables 9-1 and 9-2 are partial reports showing drill-down analysis into KM participation by region during calendar year 2000. This type of analysis had been difficult to perform until Microsoft began using Analysis Services. This type of analysis allowed them to spot and respond very quickly to different trends.

Table 9-1.   Knowledge Asset Reuse, By Region By Quarter

Region ID	Year 2000				
	Quarter 1	Quarter 2	Quarter 3	Quarter 4	Total
Adriatics	6	67	55	53	181
Alps	45	447	342	290	1,124
Andean	7	466	326	364	1,163
Asia HQ	78	199	125	43	445
Australia	62	626	690	730	2,108
Benelux	33	254	287	298	872
Brazil	15	204	130	460	809
Bulgaria	1		6		7
Canada	181	1,549	1,514	1,816	5,060
Caribbean & CA	2	224	323	273	822
Corporate	19	67	50	132	268
Czech & Slovak Republic		2	51	29	82
eCommerce	20	183	217	367	787
EMEA HQ	21	200	201	110	532

Table 9-2.   Knowledge Asset Production, By Region By Quarter

Region ID	Year 2000 Quarter 1	Quarter 2	Quarter 3	Quarter 4	Total
Adriatics				1	1
Alps	6	5	7	15	33
Andean	5	1	1	1	8
Asia HQ	1	2	14	8	25
Australia	16	26	16	49	107
Benelux	7	3	4	13	27
Brazil	3	7		75	85
Canada	16	135	31	65	247
Caribbean & CA		1			1
Corporate	2	16	31	9	58
eCommerce	7	29	12	11	59
EMEA HQ	4	10	7	14	35

Now that we have reviewed what to measure and how to capture it, let's shift gears and talk about the actual repository and the requirements for content management.

Managing Content in the Knowledge Asset Repository

We have spent some time discussing the need to measure the use and reuse of the content in the repository without talking about how it gets there. There is little mystery about the origin of KAs—they are the outflow or results of knowledge work. Thus, it is important to spend some time thinking about how knowledge workers can contribute their work.

Giving participants the ability to contribute and identify the content being submitted to a repository is an important feature requirement you should not overlook. Identifying content (that is, associating it with organizational techniques, such as taxonomy or visual maps) should make it easier to set up a content management infrastructure that supports knowledge sharing. Content management features that support users might include services (platform system and process) that facilitate creation, submission, quality assurance workflow (technical review and editing, application of standard templates), versioning, and auditing. If the initial design of your system includes a self-service feature (that is, allowing the submitter to aid in managing the content by making taxonomy or other data associations), KM content management should not tax your information technology (IT) support department and will give participants a way to collaborate on content development as well as reuse.

As defined in earlier chapters, a repository is a centralized location for the aggregation of KAs that are stored and maintained in an organized manner. Depending on how the term is used, a repository may be directly accessible to users or may be a place from which specific databases, files, or documents are obtained for further relocation or distribution in a network. A repository may be just the aggregation of data itself into some organized accessible place of storage or it may also imply some ability to selectively extract data.

Repository content management starts with the content submission form. Submitted content (KAs) represent the body of the system users' experience and learning acquired through customer engagements or created assets. The submission is done with a submission form, which is similar to a cover sheet for a fax document or a material breakdown form for a shipment. All knowledge workers who submit content to the repository need one simple submission process to use as the only means of submitting knowledge. Making it possible to submit knowledge online as well as offline can alleviate problems of convenience and performance.

The submission form, as shown in Figure 9-6, allows the user to select from the categories of taxonomy. Aligning KAs with the appropriate taxonomy, as defined in Chapter 6, helps you categorize the content for quick access through the search interface or other mapping techniques used to link the content with the knowledge seeker's needs. Optimally, submitters will fill out all fields. As an option, the system requirements should identify the key or primary taxonomy categories required by all content or groups of content (code segments may have different store tags than promotional materials, for example).

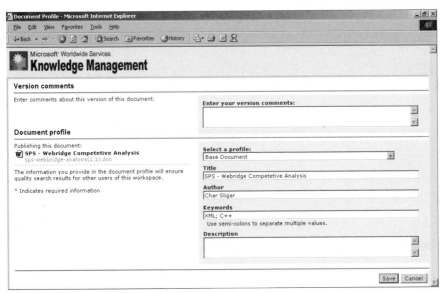

Figure 9-6.   *Sample Submission Form*

Once content is successfully categorized and submitted into the repository, it can then be managed according to the rules of the system. Content versioning is a system feature and process that allows participants to collaborate collectively on KAs. This collaboration results in different versions of an initial KA. The storage of these versions provides an "audit trail" of updates and changes made to the content, when they were made, and by whom. Versioning helps ensure that KAs evolve and that several parties review them to ensure correctness and quality.

"Check-out/check-in" is a standard method of allowing document versioning. By providing the ability to check out a KA (which locks out other users from making changes or edits while check-out is in effect), make updates, and then check the asset back in, you have a simple way to allow for content versioning.

Other business rules for the management of the content will concern updating, deleting, and archiving the content submitted to the repository. Business rules in content usage and security will need to be discussed, documented, and built into the system. Some organizations might have a class of KAs that can be freely shared with customers, a class that is reserved for business partners, and still a third class of KAs that is for internal use only. Many organizations might have a limited class of KAs that is highly guarded and visible only to the immediate team working on a specific project. You will need to carefully develop security rules before the development team builds the repository. The legal department in many businesses will need to review the classification, visibility, and security of the KA repository as well. It is good to keep in mind that you are developing a system that will hold valuable company assets.

Impact of Changing Taxonomy

It is important that metadata and the way content is classified evolve as company terminology becomes better understood. This usage and evolution plays a critical role in giving knowledge workers the ability to find the information they are looking for more easily. However, this evolution does not come without a price; the effects of changing content taxonomy, as described in Chapter 6, raise many content management issues.

When considering updating taxonomy, you need to consider several things. For example, if taxonomy metatags are removed, added, or updated, current content needs to be moved or mapped to the appropriate category. This process can be very difficult depending on the number of metadata changes that are made and how many KAs are directly affected. Technical implementation of the repository plays an important role in the overall ease or difficulty of this process.

When you are in the planning stage of a KM system and want to plan to accommodate such changes, you can consider several ways to do that. These strategies include infrastructure and processes that efficiently support taxonomy change management. Developers need to ensure that the system can evolve with the knowledge workers' business initiatives. The KM system must fit not only within the organization's IT infrastructure but also into the larger business model. This ensures that the correct infrastructure is in place for easy evolution and growth. The KM system operators (people who manage KM) need to be notified of changes in the IT infrastructure as well as of new products, services, and groups they will need to support as the business changes and grows.

Another process you can effectively manage is the gathering of a consensus on taxonomy updates and KA mapping. Ensuring that key stakeholders and appropriate individuals are involved in the process from the beginning is essential. Although this aspect is a cliché in a lot of implementation projects, it is particularly important here, especially with regard to technical personnel.

They need to fully understand what changes are being made to make this process seamless.

Although the evolution of taxonomy and metadata can be a rigorous process, it is an essential one. Precisely defining and classifying information makes it much easier to find KAs in the repository. The more customized this classification is to the organization, the more time will be saved in locating KAs when they are needed.

Summary

Collecting, organizing, and making content available are central functions of the KM repository system. Statistics on these functions, as well as on the activities in the virtual space, give employees and managers a means to determine usage, growth, and development of KAs. The role of measurement in the KM system is to ensure that data on work behaviors and KM function is delivered to the management team, who will analyze it against the established metrics and promote appropriate behaviors to improve productivity and efficiency across the organization.

Count what is known

Expose what is needed

chapter 10

Knowledge Searching and Services

The British created a civil-service job in 1803 calling for a man to stand on the Cliffs of Dover with a spyglass. He was supposed to ring a bell if he saw Napoleon coming. The job was abolished in 1945.

Gen. Michael E. Ryan, U.S. Air Force chief of staff[1]

Just as with the lookout on the Cliffs of Dover, a knowledge management (KM) system must deliver real and timely value or it should not exist. Old, inaccessible, unusable, or poorly organized knowledge assets (KAs) add little to the business and should be retired. Supporting KM users' ability to find the knowledge they need and connect with expertise is the essence of a KM system. To be effective, the KM system needs to make its KAs easy to find and retrieve. Its users need to be able to intuitively access stored knowledge and connect to experts. Searching and locating is the process that makes this discovery of information possible. In this chapter we outline strategies, not coding techniques, that aid in initiating effective repository searches, expertise locators, and general techniques for connecting the information and knowledge available throughout the enterprise (in other applications or storage media). As part of this discussion, we will point out key design and development considerations that are based on our experiences designing and developing the Microsoft Consulting Services (MCS) KM system.

What Creates Successful Searching?

An effective search considers the initial user experience. The process of searching for information needs to fit naturally with how the users work. The user's interface to the system—portal, community, or otherwise—should be organized, reliable, and easy to navigate. As a longer-term aim, searching should provide an alternate way to find information or content to allow users to consistently have relevant KAs filtered to them through an intelligent system.

---

1. From the speech "Preparing for the 21st Century," *http://www.af.mil/news/speech/current/ Preparing_for_the_21st_Cent.html.*

Finally, and more simply, a successful search should return the KAs that the users are looking for consistently and predictably. The following sections discuss how search methods for KM are constructed and what key components you may want to focus on as you explore KM systems.

The Technology of Searching

The backbone of every search is a **search engine**. In broad terms, a search engine bridges the gap between the user interface and the data store or repository. It brings the content to the user by indexing the assets that are stored and returning the assets when they are asked for. Search engines can be set up to index, or **crawl** (seek out content by keyword or phrase and link it to search results), content in a wide array of locations. For example, content stored in a database, in a file share, on the Internet, or on a corporate intranet site can be indexed or crawled and returned as a result set.

To further understand how search engines work, it is important to become familiar with the major search features and terms, such as free-text search, attribute search, and advanced search, so that you can determine the best search to meet your specific needs. Keep in mind that search technology continues to evolve and will most likely change over the life of your KM system.

Before moving into a discussion of search features, it is a good idea to review the components that enable discoverability:

- **Search engine.**   The subsystem that supports searching of content and domains of content distributed over an intranet.

- **Information architecture.**   A model of how the system could make inferences based on tagging (taxonomy) and a model of how content can be grouped or aggregated into related collections.

- **Content delivery.**   The application portal, its application servers, and Web servers

- **Profiling and personalization services.**   The programmatic efforts and platform system support to identify users and target content delivery or provide application customization.

Kinds of Searches

A search engine is a service that indexes, organizes, and often reviews and rates content. It helps you find the one needle you are looking for in the haystack. Different search techniques work in different ways:

- Some rely on people to maintain an index of sites or pages.

- Some use software to identify key information on sites across the intranet (internal) or the Internet (external).

- Some combine both types of service.

KM system developers preselect one or more techniques to present to the KM user. In the following section we will review some of the most common search techniques.

Free-Text Searches

Free-text searches are ones in which the user can enter any set of words, phrases, or even a complete sentence to return a result set. The system looks at the text and identifies all the nouns and noun phrases in it. The search engine determines how the free-text query is processed and the result set returned. For example, Figure 10-1 shows the request and results for a free-text search calling for documents relating to "Exchange Deployment." It is interesting to note that in order to retrieve documents containing both terms ("Exchange" and "Deployment") the user is required to enclose the text in quotation marks. Without the quotation marks, the search engine would return results containing references to "Exchange" or "Deployment," or both terms.

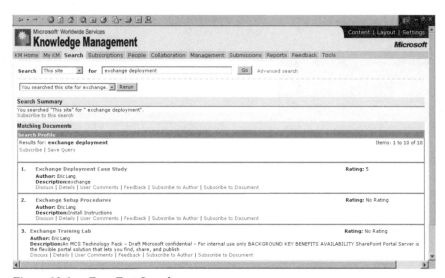

Figure 10-1.   *Free-Text Search*

Attribute or Taxonomy-Based Searches

Search engines can index KAs by the tags that are stored when the assets are submitted. Taxonomy (or properties such as author, category, or keyword) plays a key role in aiding the search process. This means that KA submitters have a direct influence over how the content is categorized and what content description appears when that content comes up in the search engine hit.

See Also   You can find more information about taxonomies in Chapter 6, "Building Taxonomies," and details on content classification in Chapter 7, "Capturing Your Organization's Knowledge Assets."

Advanced Searches

Using both tags and free text can help users find content more accurately. Such a combination is usually presented as an **advanced search** (see Figure 10-2) that allows the user to qualify several criteria before making a query. Advanced searches often allow the user to add criteria such as location or version numbers to product requests. This qualification, sometimes called an operator, allows a smaller, more accurate result set to be returned.

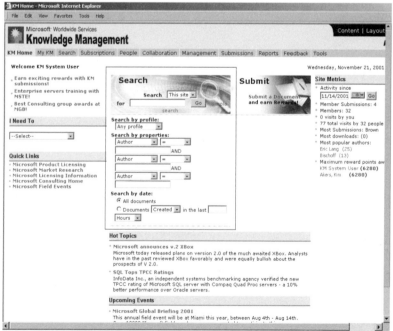

Figure 10-2.   *Advanced Search*

Taxonomy, date range, and language are examples of common operators that can be used in an advanced search form. For example, a user might specify documents by a specific author or language. Value and author are other effective attributes that can be made available through advanced searches.

Visual Navigation of Structured Content

To make it easier to discover your organization's KAs, you might want to implement **visual browsing** of the content repository—through a mechanism like the knowledge index (KI) described in Chapter 7. In typical searching methods, a knowledge worker must describe to some extent what he or she is looking for. But sometimes a knowledge worker is not able to describe or name what he or she is looking for. Visual browsing helps the user by providing an interface that names and organizes the repository's contents. This reduces the need to understand the taxonomy and provides a free-form means to discover what is in the repository.

As your repository grows, your system should incorporate some structure to group content into logical categories. A simple structure that most people can relate to is the book/section/chapter analogy described in Chapter 7. The book could represent a technology, engagement, or customer type. Sections could represent different phases of a project or engagement or technology version, and chapters would focus on the details.

Another benefit of visual navigation is that it makes content gaps or surpluses obvious. Gap analysis is very important in determining what KAs people want or need but which are missing from the repository. This is very similar to analyzing search requests that return zero assets. On the plus side, it becomes obvious that you either do not need to collect further assets in this category and or it is time to perform some content cleanup and determine which are the most valuable assets to retain or bubble to the top and which should be considered for retirement.

To support structured navigation, you may need to expand the system by adding terms or categories to the existing taxonomy. If your existing taxonomy supports a hierarchical structure (that is, book/section/chapter), no changes are needed at first. You may want to add additional taxonomy elements to support structured viewing from different perspectives. There is limited value to visual browsing of a large linear list, as there is no "grouping." Linear browsing of shorter lists may be fine, such as a list of validated KAs for a given technology. (See the MCS KM example later in this chapter.)

In addition to the taxonomy-supported internal structure, the client (user) side of the program needs to support viewing such a visual structure. You can build a fat client where some of the processing is performed on the client or use a thin client where all of the process is performed at the server. The thin client (where the server does not send large amounts of code or data to the local machine) has advantages for mobile and remote users. Due to the volatility and expense of modem connectivity, these users require the most compact code, the smallest possible download packages, and the fastest search methods available. These remote KM users are one of the greatest challenges to a KM system.

The Repository Knowledge Index screen shown in Figure 10-3 provides an example of visual navigation. To support the way consultants wanted to view and group content, additional taxonomy terms were added to support hierarchical grouping of content. Each technology community created one or more "books" for grouping KAs and then applied additional taxonomy to support the grouping.

For displaying this index, the MCS KM tool used a tree structure control and color-coding to represent different content types. At a given level within the tree display, if content was available, the title, author, number of downloads, and document rating information is displayed. When a user selects a document, the document abstract is displayed. Once these key elements of the document have been viewed, the user has the option to open the document or request that it be sent through e-mail. Visual mapping techniques, such as the MCS KM knowledge index, allow users to quickly identify what information is available on a topic. Missing KAs are quickly identified on visual maps by highlighting the gaps through color-coding, empty box symbols, or other visual indicators that the user will readily identify.

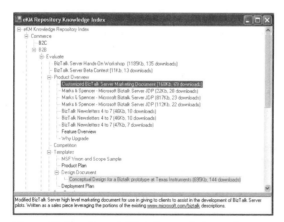

Figure 10-3.   *Sample Visual Knowledge Index*

Returning Optimal Results

The obvious goal of any search engine is to return the best result set. Most search engines return the result set by weighing rank and relevancy. In other words, the KAs that are returned are sorted according to how closely they match the query. But it is challenging to make this result set applicable to the users if the taxonomy is not closely aligned to the user's thinking. Sometimes the taxonomy is good, but the KA is either too complex (covers too many subject areas) to fit neatly into the taxonomy categories or is on a subject area the taxonomy does not yet cover.

How did Microsoft handle this? The MCS KM team at Microsoft categorized highly reusable assets and called these assets "Gems." Knowledge Gems (or validated KAs, as discussed in Chapter 7) represent the best work the field consultants have produced in regard to a particular problem or deliverable. To be classified as a Gem in the MCS KM system, a subject matter expert (SME) must review and approve the KA. Validated KAs, such as Gems, should have specific preset characteristics such as being:

- Highly reusable for similar work
- Validated through use or experience
- Highly sanitized (customer-ready) for quick reuse with any customer

The search process was set up to rank validated KAs as more relevant content to users by moving all results that are tagged as validated to the top of the result set. This in turn provided easiest access to the assets that were viewed collectively by the field as having the most relevant application to doing their job and saving them time.

You can also optimize the result set by extending the key searching features. You might use an extended data repository search, saved searches, and viewable feedback. Extended data repositories, for example, give users the ability to search a Microsoft Exchange public folder where e-mail archives can be found. Microsoft SharePoint Portal Server has built-in capabilities to handle this functionality across predefined distribution lists.

Although returning the optimal result set can be challenging, it is an essential part in getting knowledge workers to use the system. When KAs can be quickly and consistently accessed, you aid discoverability and encourage asset submissions, too. If knowledge workers are confident that their assets can be easily found and reused, they are initially more likely to submit the information.

Personalization

As mentioned previously, your search system will have to evolve. How well it evolves depends on how well the KM planners and developers understand the system's users. The more you know about the user, the more knowledge you can collectively "push" to the user, and the better you can discard random or irrelevant information.

Personas and portal application personalization techniques can help you customize content delivery for your users. A persona gives users a complete personalized view of the KM system. Key elements of this view can include

- The most popular documents and experts that are relevant to the projects that the user is working on

- A list of most recent downloads made by the user

- A list of subscriptions made by the user

- Customizable popular links for the user

- Documents submitted by the user that are pending approval before being published in the KM system

- Links to update the user's personal, skill, and project profile

To better explain this approach, we will use the MCS KM system as an example. The MCS KM team already knew that Microsoft consultants were the users of their system. Therefore, they were able to collect large amounts of significant data on these individuals. Most of this data was standard information like location, practice, and office—all information stored in human resources (HR) databases. Other information based on the consultants' work (such as job title or training) was accessible through another remote database. Collectively, this information helped the team create a base profile on each individual who accessed the system based on their unique logon ID. Based on the profile and the community, the consultant selected to associate with the system could present a unique mix of KAs tailored to each consultant.

Through the user interface, as shown in Figure 10-4, MCS consultants were given the ability to quickly customize their profiles (by editing their profiles on the Web site after they log on the first time) and save the changes. The accuracy of the profile attributes evolved to the point where content could be appropriately "pushed" to the user. When an MCS consultant accessed the system, he or she was presented with a view of all KAs that were relevant to his or her profile. These assets came in the form of relevant repository submissions, knowledge Gems, existing experts, and community information.

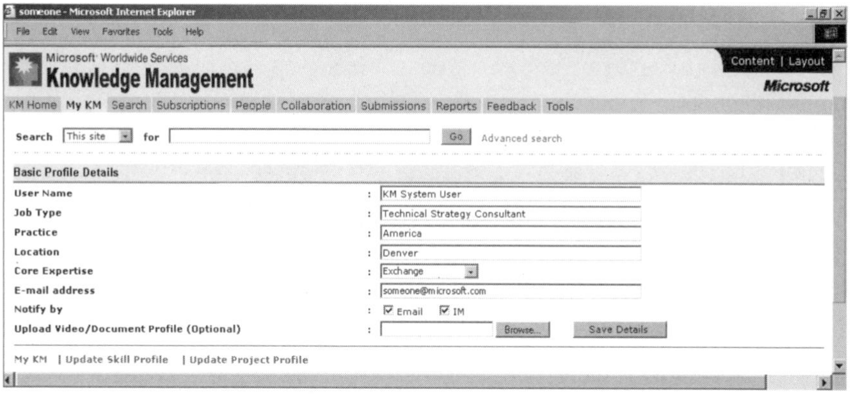

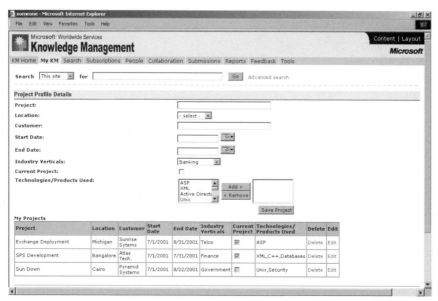

Figure 10-4. *Interface of Persona*

You can extend the persona process, as shown in Figure 10-5, to capture other vital information from users on current projects and engagements. You can build on this information to provide up-to-date content in the form of KAs, projects, and experts that are relevant to the individual's current status—all of which you can use to push knowledge to the users that in turn makes them work more intelligently and successfully.

Figure 10-5. *Interface Example of Adding Project/Engagement Information to Persona*

Subscription and Notification Services

Subscription services ensure that system users are constantly up-to-date on changes or updates made to information relevant to them. Subscription notification (not just for magazines or newsletters) is an excellent way to deliver customized updates on assets, individuals, and even services.

A KM system should allow a user to subscribe to as many or as few of its resources that the user deems necessary, as shown in Figure 10-6. When a user has a subscription, the user receives notification when a change occurs in any of the subscribed KM resources.

Figure 10-6. *Collective Personalized View and Delivery of Content*

Some of the standard subscriptions that can be supported include

- Subscribe to Authors (Notify user if the author of any selected document posts a new document)

- Subscribe to Documents (Notify user if a new version of any selected document is submitted to the KM system)

- Subscribe to Experts (Notify user if the profile of any selected expert changes)
- Subscribe to Searches (Notify user if there are new documents to any subscribed search query)

Finding Experts

Technology enables the KM system to join information collected in different parts of the enterprise (such as HR or Finance). If structured properly, this union of data can identify expertise across the enterprise and connect people with people. These expert finder systems provide yet another information resource to users based on known criteria about skills or experience. This information facilitates peer-to-peer communication.

For the KM system user, an expert finding service should work like any other search routine within the KM system, as shown in Figure 10-7. The example given in Figure 10-7 shows a people search query with the keyword "Exchange" and the filter "Experts" returning a list of all Exchange experts in the organization. As we will discuss in the next few pages, this function is potentially very complex and reaches far beyond the KM system's boundaries. Regardless of the technology and reach of this service, the user should not be required to have specific knowledge of the external (to KM) systems being searched. In other words, the KM system must provide a simple-to-use finder service to the user. Once this expert finder service has located one or more candidate experts, the requestor (KM system user) needs to quickly develop some level of confidence that he or she has truly located the right people. One way to quickly establish this confidence is to allow the user to learn more about the expertise of the experts by clicking the link associated with them. This link would provide additional information about the candidate experts and might include information such as past projects, industries they have worked in (such as health care or automotive), technologies they have used, their level of proficiency in each of the technologies, and possibly even a video profile. The expert profile may show the KAs and electronic conversations (as we will discuss in the section of this chapter entitled "Programmatic Expert Determination") and the rating (by other users) of this evidence.

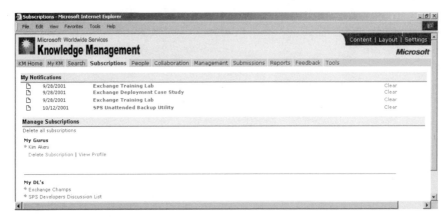

Figure 10-7. *Interface Example of Expertise Finder System*

Additionally, the page could display the expert's availability on Instant Messaging (IM). A KM system user could potentially add the expert to his or her buddy list for discussions later or immediately contact the expert by IM, if he or she is available online. This is a very rich area of KM that is just beginning to surface as the technology to support it, as a seamless service, is emerging.

Determining Expertise

For expert finder systems to effectively present knowledge workers with "expert" candidates, the system first needs to be able to determine who those experts are. There are two main ways of determining expertise: manually or programmatically. Although both ways have advantages and disadvantages, you will need to determine the appropriate approach for your own business.

Manual Expert Determination

The manual process starts with knowledge workers rating or categorizing *themselves* as "experts" with regards to products, solutions, competencies, or other information that the organization can use to classify them. This information is then stored in a data table for access and updating. Figure 10-8 shows the form that users might fill out in the case of a manually run expert determination process. As you can see, the knowledge workers enter the system and record the level of their expertise with regard to organizational focus areas. This information is then saved and stored for access by other knowledge workers to view. This is the starting point for expertise finding and can be combined with programmatic expert finding. Many KM systems we have reviewed in our study of the subject provide this simple (self-declaration) level of expert finding, often combining it with user rating of experts. It is a good start and should not be discounted. We are currently seeing the enabling technology emerge that will allow the KM system to cross-check and refine the expert identification process. In many cases the true experts in your organization do not have the time to self-declare their expertise (or may see this as egotistical). They are often the most focused or the busiest people in your organization—you need noninvasive measures of expertise (requiring little or no intervention by the person being measured) that the identified expert can confirm or deny.

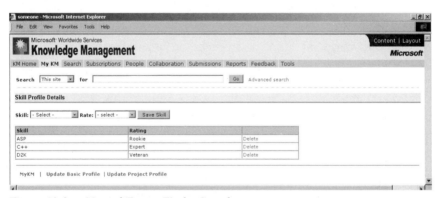

Figure 10-8. *Manual Expert Finder Search*

Programmatic Expert Determination

If a KM system is set up to handle noninvasive expert determination, it can lessen the knowledge worker's and the expert's time and effort to both find and confirm expertise. You can implement many approaches, from the simplest links to complex services, to accomplish programmatic expert determination. The Netscan program at *http://netscan.research.Microsoft.com/* is an example of a complex programmatic implementation in the Public Space.

As discussed in Chapter 9, "Measuring the Effectiveness of Your Repository," the Netscan program collects information from community-based electronic conversations (e-mail or other threaded conversations) and analyzes the data to help the user determine who might be able to answer the question. It can also place a confidence rating on the response the user receives, as discussed in Chapter 8, "Building a KM Foundation," in the section entitled "Implementation Stage." Microsoft uses Netscan technology to help users find and determine expertise within Microsoft's USENET communities.

As mentioned earlier, Netscan is a set of software tools being developed through Microsoft Research that are designed to aid in the sociological study of the Internet. It works by collecting baseline measures of a USENET community (its structure and dynamics) to produce a map of the kinds and qualities of the groups and institutions that form when people use the Internet to interact with one another. Netscan provides a range of measures of activity in the various Microsoft USENET communities, including the number of messages in each of the groups studied and the number of people who participate in them. Some interesting patterns can emerge when this data is analyzed over a period of hours, days, weeks, or longer. You can also study other network media like e-mail lists, chat rooms, and proprietary discussion systems in this way. Netscan is one example of noninvasive programmatic expert determination. New tools are emerging in this area of KM all the time. We expect to see continual improvement in the enabling technology in this area for quite some time.

The Netscan statistical analysis of persistent conversations works by entering the name of a newsgroup the user is interested in into the system. This returns a result set of all matching newsgroups. When the user selects a newsgroup, Netscan generates a custom report for the newsgroup for the time period selected.

Netscan is really two tools. First, the Netscan collector connects to a USENET News (Network News Transfer Protocol [NNTP]) server that carries thousands of newsgroups (over 90,000 at our last count) and collects all the messages in all the newsgroups. Netscan reads all these messages and stores selected information drawn from the message header. It constructs and maintains a database of this information. The second part of Netscan, the analyzer, can read selected portions of this database to generate reports and analyses of selected newsgroups over selected periods of time. The ultimate goal is to shed light on the vast invisible continent of social cyberspace and to see the crowds that are gathered there and, within those crowds, analyze who is asking and who is answering. You can use Netscan, or similar technology, to analyze internal electronic conversation threads to expose and reward currently hidden expertise.

.NET and Knowledge Management

A key point we have referenced over the previous three chapters is the need to *link* your KM system with other applications relating to the management of intellectual capital, such as HR, resource management, and learning. We emphasize the word *link* to point out that even hinting at rebuilding or replacing these infrastructure applications would be fiscally and practically unwise for most companies. Your technology team can use many techniques to accomplish this task; Microsoft advocates the use of its .NET technology to link and integrate all your existing intellectual capital processes with KM. In Chapter 8 we described a three-tier KM architecture. Tier 2 of that architecture calls for the implementation of business rules, metadata, and the integration of diverse sources of data to present to the client (tier 1). Tier 2 of this architecture is where the benefits of the .NET approach can best be realized. .NET was designed to encapsulate diverse applications and present them in a uniform fashion to the client (tier 1) layer. The .NET approach is composed of unique services and languages that make application and user connectivity simple and customizable.

Before presenting you with a KM Expert Finder example of a .NET service, we will take you quickly through the .NET concept. The .NET platform includes a comprehensive family of products, built on industry Extensible Markup Language (XML) and Internet standards, that provides for each aspect of developing (tools), managing (servers), using (building block services and smart clients), and experiencing (rich user experiences) XML Web services. .NET will potentially integrate the applications, tools, and servers you may already use today. Figure 10-9, "KM Expert Finder Web Service Diagram," is a graphical representation of a potential KM Expert Finder function developed with .NET components. Once again, we should remind the reader that this is a very high-level and simplistic representation of the technology. As we discuss the various .NET components in Table 10-1, we will refer to this diagram to help you visualize how .NET could work within a KM environment.

Table 10-1.   .NET Components

.NET Term	Description
Web services	A Web service is a module of application logic that can be published, discovered, and executed over the Web (or intranet) using XML-based standards. These **XML-based Web services** (the numbered items in Figure 10-9), which developers can customize for use in any Web environment, are a part of the Microsoft .NET programming model. The .NET platform enables the creation and use of XML-based applications, processes, and Web sites as Web services. Web services share and combine information and functionality with each other by design, on any platform or smart device (such as a Web phone or palm computer), to provide tailored solutions for organizations and individuals. Building on a common programming model and drawing on a wealth of prebuilt components and services lets developers devote more time to creating reusable business logic components and less time to working on the underlying maintenance code necessary for all applications. In Microsoft .NET, the infrastructure is built on the idea that computing is moving away from the era of isolated PCs and servers, packaged software, and disconnected "islands" of data in databases and on Web sites. (See the description of individual KM Expert Finder Web services in Figure 10-9 following this table.)
XML	XML, or Extensible Markup Language, is a format for structuring data on the Web. XML implements rules for formatting data in such a way that it is easy for a computer to read created files.
SOAP	Simple Object Access Protocol (SOAP) is built on XML. It makes it possible for applications to call each other in a standard, loosely coupled way, which makes it possible to build applications that are distributed across the Internet. If you think of the interactions between XML Web services as a phone call, XML describes the things that applications say to each other in their conversations; SOAP describes how they call each other on the phone. How do you greet the service at the other end? ("Hello?") How do you ask for something? For example, in Figure 10-9 the Locating Service (#2) uses SOAP as a standardized method for getting location information (on the registered or available services) from the Registry (of information) based on the request made by the user.
UDDI	If XML is the conversation and SOAP describes the rules on how you call someone, Universal Description, Discovery, and Integration (UDDI) is the phone book. UDDI provides a directory of XML Web services, which allows you to find applications (or external businesses) that offer XML Web services.

Figure 10-9 shows five Web services connecting the user request to the registry of services (UDDI) and the applications (providing information) in a sample environment. These services are:

1. **Publishing service.**   Establishes that a Web entity (internal or external) is available. For example, a skills database from the learning organization may publish that it can identify experts.

2. **Locating service.**   Provides filtered connectivity—that is, it takes the search request to the UDDI to obtain a subset of data (based on the request parameters). UDDI provides service calling information in SOAP format from the Publishing Service.

3. **Calling service.**   Provides to the requestor all known service options available (at this time) to satisfy the request.

4. **Invoke service.**   Allows the requestor to execute (or actually find experts) based on the returned subset of information provided by the calling service.

5. **Execute service.**   Brings back the selected experts for review.

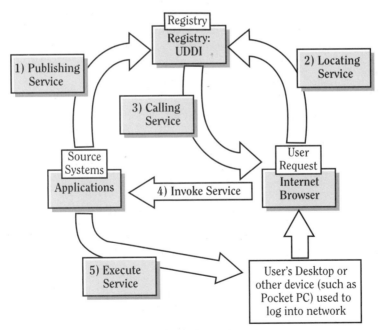

Figure 10-9.   *KM Expert Finder Web Service Diagram*

KM Utilization of Web Services

Any systems across a company, from KM to HR or accounting databases, can be available as Web services that communicate and share data using common Internet standards such as XML and SOAP. These services can then be combined with other Web services (internally or externally). In the diagram shown in Figure 10-9, the KM system is using a .NET service to enhance its expert finding capabilities. Information regarding the participant's skills may be lodged in the training groups database, while the person's experience information may reside in the HR database. The KM system may know what topics the participant has contributed against (as either in the KA repository as described in Chapter 7 or in a persistent electronic conversation as described earlier in this section) and the rated value (by other users) of that content. Combining all this information through a .NET service would allow the KM system to build a true picture of the participant's expertise.

These aspects, when integrated into the programmable logic of a KM system, can clearly provide benefits by integrating external (to KM) source information dynamically with internal KM information. This approach transforms the logic into reusable components that can be published and consumed through secure interactions across secured boundaries. .NET effectively allows systems to "talk" to one another, thus removing artificial application layer barriers and facilitating the flow of knowledge within an enterprise.

Locate the experience

Link the enterprise

Conclusion

There will come a time when you believe everything is
finished. That will be the beginning.

Louis L'Amour, Lonely on the Mountain

Knowledge Management Means Good Business

Knowledge management (KM) is gradually taking hold in the business world as the key component to unlocking the enterprise's intellectual capital. Companies recognize, more than ever, that business is about value. In today's knowledge economy, it is not just basic business transactions that determine corporate value. Intangible asset growth, such as successful test results for a software program or a new medication, creates market value. Supporting, promoting, and valuing the intellectual and human capital that produce profitability are the primary business challenges of this decade. More and more companies are meeting the new challenges by learning how to fuel the knowledge engine that powers twenty-first-century business with shared information, experience, and know-how.

In this book we have shown that sharing knowledge among workers is the lifeline of any knowledge-based enterprise. KM is the means by which an enterprise gathers, organizes, shares, and analyzes the knowledge of individuals and groups across the organization to directly affect performance. KM is about urging and enabling people to communicate, exchange, and share information. To paraphrase a popular saying in the KM world, KM is the process and structure for getting the right information, in the right format, to the right person, at the right time, for the right business purpose.

It is now essential for a company to unlock its information for knowledge workers so that they have the right data and information to make sound business decisions and to innovate. The changes that the rapid pace of knowledge growth are driving are often stressful, but transforming the world into a knowledge economy is a revolutionary step in economic history. When businesses focus only on physical assets, growth is limited to the quantity (such as inventory or land) of those assets. But knowledge that is applied to the issues and challenges facing the world not only makes better use of the physical assets available to us but also can free us from physical work and allow human potential to expand.

Knowledge has an unlimited capacity for renewal; it is expandable, self-generating, transportable, and shareable. In essence, it is the ultimate resource if it is managed, channeled, and supported. People can use their knowledge to create technology, and that technology can support innovation that in turn can create better technology. These new ideas and technology are translated into a more effective business that is capable of increasing productivity. The greater the productivity in an organization, the greater the potential for profit.

The cultural changes that this shift implies are not always easy. KM promises no quick answers or simple fixes to complex business problems. It requires people running companies and people working in companies to change how they think as well as how they work. It requires us to change our ways—no longer can we hoard resources, information, or solutions in our department. Change is not easy. It cannot be accomplished with pep rallies, declarations of good intent by senior management, or flashy posters in the hallways.

Although we have discussed the management of knowledge at some length, we have only opened the conversation. We have only introduced the concepts of organizational change management and performance management. These two issues alone are the subjects of many books. But uncertainty about these issues is not a reason to put off what must be done to stay competitive. Launching a successful KM initiative requires coordinating the environment (including people), processes, and technology components that are unique to every organization. It starts with a solid business strategy and requires not only technology and communication enablers but a long-term commitment to sustaining a knowledge-empowered environment—that is, an environment that supports and encourages the work behaviors of sharing, reuse, and communication of knowledge and experience. Engage your team, explore the issues, and start a plan.

- Challenge your managers—make KM part of their objectives
- Challenge the business—make the Knowledge Value Assessment a requirement
- Challenge your company—reward KM behavior and activities

This book has been about change. Over the past half-century we have experienced the most rapid period of social, economic, and technological changes in the history of humankind. Change is now measured in hours and days rather than in years and decades. Basic business structures are changing and require a new approach. Knowledge workers—people who produce value from the efforts of their minds rather than from physical labor—are the key to our business success. This requires change in our business culture and attitudes. If knowledge truly grows, as we have stated, through collaboration, the knowledge-era company must support, enhance, and promote a sharing culture. In such an environment, technology is a primary enabler of KM. It provides the foundation for solutions that automate and centralize the sharing of knowledge and fueling of the innovative process. A KM system should be designed to ensure that technology issues enable, not encumber, a corporation's efforts in this area.

Throughout this book we have emphasized five focal points for the culture that are enabled by technology:

Share tacit knowledge by collaborating.   The integrated collaborative capabilities of current technologies such as Microsoft Office XP and Microsoft SharePoint Portal Server allow users to innovate together within their familiar desktop environments. Sharing calendars, tasks, threaded discussions, documents, home pages, and a repository helps groups collaborate and move knowledge from the Personal to the Corporate Space. The connectivity enhanced by electronic conferencing software, like Microsoft NetMeeting, contains tools such as electronic white-boarding, video, chat, and application-sharing that allow users not only to communicate but also to work together on knowledge assets (KAs) as they collaborate, regardless of location.

Connect knowledge through teams and communities.   Teams and communities across an organization can help provide information and encourage reuse of information. Technology-enabled techniques such as personalization, advanced search techniques, and collaborative workflow methods, which are available in solutions like SharePoint Portal Server, help to create such groups. Tracking these behaviors and activities allows companies to identify best practices by measuring successes, while workflow tools enable the creation of process-based applications to ensure that the practices are followed and measured. By building on a common taxonomy with workflow tools and shared KAs, a company supports the evolution of the business asset base and speeds up searching and overall knowledge delivery effectiveness.

Manage explicit knowledge to make it useful for others.   Content management technologies allow people to capture, codify, and organize experiences and ideas in central repositories that offer seamless, intuitive access to the entire organization. The seamless integration of the familiar desktop with the power of a database-driven repository gives the knowledge worker the ability to categorize, publish, and manage all forms of KAs, from documents and programming code to multimedia files. Electronic storage and retrieval are no longer limited to simple text files and keyword searches.

Measure what you manage.   Being able to spot trends in financial and business data allows decision makers to plan better strategies. The data-warehousing and business intelligence analysis functions built into many of today's technology solutions help knowledge workers better understand the trends within their business, see the flow of knowledge across groups, and spot areas for improvement or innovation. The ability to capture and analyze cross-enterprise data from accounting, human resources, learning, and KM systems today allows management to have a transparent view of an entire organization. Microsoft online analytical processing (OLAP) tools, dynamic views, and Office Web Services allow users to easily analyze vast amounts of data in their familiar Office or browser environments. KM knowledge behavior tracking methods, such as Microsoft's innovative Netscan tools, enable KM participants and managers not only to see the use of the system but also to track persistent conversations, find expertise, and locate answers quickly through statistical analysis. Correlating results data to KM behavioral data gives managers and knowledge workers the information they need to change how they do business and increase productivity.

Build on a solid foundation.   As with all systems, a solid and reliable foundation is a critical success factor. Building the KM solution on a solid organizational and technological foundation is the first step. To ensure success, it is critical to design both the corporate culture and the technology to scale as the business grows, to meet the challenges of competition, and to ensure that activities are carried out in a timely manner. Plan for success, maintain for stability, and allow for change. Remember:

Knowledge is static

Knowing is dynamic

Innovation requires both

The Future of Knowledge Management

The emphasis of knowledge exchange is shifting. Although corporate information exchange used to be limited to just personal use or peer-to-peer sharing within departments, it is fast becoming a more free-flowing global process. In the near future, we will see KM practices becoming the foundation of the changing business landscape. Business leaders will shape the company cultures to be more conducive to KM, and technology will help employees more easily reuse information in a world of escalating connectivity.

The capacity to turn knowing into knowledge and knowledge into productivity and innovation will be the hallmark of the successful enterprise in the twenty-first century. The Industrial Revolution is giving way to the Knowledge Revolution. The stage is set, the players are moving into place, and the script is being written by those who see the new vision. In many ways this will be a quiet revolution—no gunfire, no loud machines, no armies of workers marching into the cities. Managing an organization in the knowledge era will become synonymous with managing all forms of knowledge. The rules of the game will evolve—the principles of good management will become synonymous with the principles of KM.

Organizational foundations are static

The future is dynamic

Glossary

activities and behaviors   In the KVA framework, the actual things people do and the ways in which that work is accomplished.

activity   In the KVA framework, a task that employees are assigned to do.

advanced search   A search that allows the user to identify several search criteria before making a query. For queries about software products, for example, advanced searches allow the user to add criteria such as location or version numbers.

asset   In KM, property that is owned by an organization.

author   In KM, a person who is a knowledge producer—that is, someone who writes or creates a piece of information that is to be included in the database of knowledge that an organization keeps.

behavior   In the KVA framework, the way in which people work, or how they perform an assigned activity.

behavioral indicator   In the KVA framework, the occurrence of a behavior that enhances the value of corporate assets.

bottom-up   A grassroots approach to solving a problem. The initiative starts by addressing a specific business problem, in a specific business unit, and later moves upward to the management level.

business unit scorecard   A report card for a business group that reflects the elements in its vitality report. *See also* vitality reports

classification   An organization system structured by defined principles of composition and purpose.

Community Knowledge Space   The environment where tacit-to-explicit knowledge conversion occurs. It is the shared exploration quadrant.

community of practice (CoP)   A group of people who share common experiences, lessons learned, and knowledge assets in a commonly defined or unified area of interest. Communities provide participants with reassurance, continuity, and structure regardless of the members' location, rank, or expertise.

community profile   A document that spells out how a community is aligned with the business objective. The profile states the community's focus and describes how to perpetuate the membership and structure the community.

content   In KM, a unique knowledge asset of any type, such as a document, diagram, multimedia file, or code sample.

content download   In KM, the act of transferring a copy of a knowledge asset from a KM repository to a user's local computer.

content management (CM)   In KM, oversight of the creation, submission, quality assurance workflow, versioning, and auditing of knowledge assets.

content submission   In KM, the act of putting forward a knowledge asset to the KM repository for consideration or review.

Corporate Knowledge Space   The environment where explicit-to-explicit knowledge exchange occurs. It is the collaborative quadrant.

countercultural change   A change that departs dramatically from the current culture.

crawl   To seek out content by keyword or phrase and add matching content to search results. Crawling is a function built into most search engines.

culture The behaviors and attitudes that define a group, company, or organization.

data management vocabulary   A taxonomy that is a short list of authorized terms without any hierarchical structure, used to support business transactions.

data mining   Searching through thousands of data records to uncover patterns and relationships contained within the activity and history store to fill a reporting request.

digital dashboard   A framework for creating a flexible portal that consolidates diverse information (personal, team, corporate, and external) into a single browser-based interface.

editor   In KM, a knowledge worker who edits content in the repository. Editing might include reviewing for message consistency, ensuring that the most significant content is brought to the audience's attention, and directing the audience to important events in the business process.

explicit   In KM, manifested physically, such as knowledge. *See also* tacit

explicit knowledge   In KM, the physical manifestation of knowledge, including white papers, information sheets, diagrams, code, and other tangible representations of the understanding and information held by people. *See also* tacit knowledge

free-text search   A search in which the user can enter any set of words, phrases, or even a complete sentence to return a result set. *See also* advanced search, visual browsing

gap analysis   A study of the difference between what is known and what should be—the gap between "as is" and "to be." A gap analysis can be an informal assessment or a formal cataloging of knowledge assets.

human capital   The ability of people to generate business value, measured in terms of tangible revenue, their ability to leverage other intangible assets, or both.

intangible asset   In KM, an asset that represent the collective knowledge, creativity, and innovative power of a company's workforce. This includes the skills, experiences, data, and supporting processes that create the knowledge (understanding, writings, diagrams, and so on), services, and products of a company. *See also* tangible asset

intellectual property (IP)   Work produced by human intellect.

KM Value Assessment (KVA) framework   An approach to understanding and measuring the value of effective KM in an organization. The KVA framework ties people's activities (things they are assigned to do), behaviors (how they perform the activities assigned), and performance goals (measurable targets linked to the company's strategic goals) in one view or value chain. The results of a KVA analysis allow a business to determine the impact of a given value chain (combination of work activities and behaviors) on profitability or production.

knowledge asset (KA)   Any learned information that is owned by an individual or by a knowledge-creating company. This can include such things as project plans, architectural diagrams, meeting transcripts, code samples, and formal and informal documentation.

knowledge index (KI)   A navigational tool that helps users identify and guide the knowledge requirements for their organization. It is arranged like a table of contents or the index of a book to help structure content so that information is easy to recognize and find.

knowledge management (KM)   The end-to-end process of revealing and mapping work activities, behaviors, and knowledge sources within an organization.

knowledge management (KM) system   The technology enabler that supports and manages the collection, distribution, collaboration and reuse of knowledge assets. Complete KM solutions include technology support for knowledge development, generation, and management of both tacit and explicit activities.

knowledge source   The location, person, or object where information comes from, such as meetings, interactions, white papers, code, or diagrams.

layered repository   Knowledge assets in a KM data store that are stratified by value, security level, and/or other criteria that limit or control access by user role (such as employee, partner, customer, or administrator).

metadata   Common words used to describe an object for information retrieval.

needs assessment   An analysis of what information is needed to perform a task or what knowledge is needed to solve problems.

persistent conversation   Correspondence in a newsgroup or e-mail distribution list that can take place over many days or months and with many people. Items or articles are posted online and are shown with all follow-up articles, the follow-ups to the follow-ups, and so on. Also called a threaded conversation.

persona   The characteristics of a group or role (such as all engineers or project managers). Individual personas act very much like information filtering in reverse. Profiles of user roles are built based on interests or functions of the aggregate group representing the role. A KM system can in turn serve people identified as belonging to a specified persona with all information associated with that persona.

Personal Knowledge Space   The environment where tacit-to-tacit knowledge exchange occurs. It is the personal discovery quadrant.

Public Knowledge Space   The environment where explicit-to-tacit knowledge exchange occurs. It is the research and investigation quadrant.

query term expansion   A synonym process in which a search engine expands a user's query to include variant forms of the term specified.

repository   In KM, a database for storing information.

search engine   A software mechanism that compares a keyword or phrase to words in Hypertext Markup Language (HTML) files that exist on the designated target such as the Internet, intranet, or KM repository, resulting in a list of responses that might relate to the keyword or phrase.

search results   In KM, the set of knowledge assets returned by the search engine provided by the KM system.

semistructured information   Information that is organized in some way—perhaps stored in a systematic way in group files or on company servers. *See also* unstructured information

site visit   A unique occurrence of a user accessing a Web page.

Special Interest Group (SIG)   A subgroup formed within a community to explore a specialized area of interest.

tacit   Implied, known, or done, but not expressed. *See also* explicit

tacit knowledge   In KM, knowledge that is known but not expressed in a physical form by a knowledge worker, such as experiences, conversations, collaboration, and learning. *See also* explicit knowledge

tag   A label assigned to data, such as formatted specifications about a document.

tangible asset   In KM, an asset that is owned by a company, such as cash, equipment, and physical inventory. *See also* intangible asset

taxonomy   In KM, a commonly understood classification of products, services, or information that can help users find knowledge in a KM solution.

team collaboration application (TCA)   A very basic version of a KM system that permits small groups to collaborate, share, and store documents.

thesaurus model   A taxonomy structure that designates preferred or authorized terms with entry terms or variants.

threaded conversation   *See* persistent conversation

top-down   A general management approach to solving a problem. The initiative starts at an organization's top management level and later moves downward to lower levels.

unstructured information   Information stored according to the desires or needs of individuals, such as on personal hard disks or on local servers. *See also* semistructured information

value-based knowledge management   An approach to knowledge management that attributes a portion of the company profit (or productivity) to KM.

value chain   In KM, a combination of work activities and behaviors. In the KVA framework, it ties people's activities (things they are assigned to do), behaviors (how they perform the activities assigned), and performance goals in one view.

visual browsing   Using a visible organization interface such as a knowledge index to discover knowledge assets within a repository.

vitality reports   Statistical trends about the health of the community. Vitality reports summarize data about individuals, business units, and community activities by specified time periods. Examples of statistics in vitality reports are: global submissions, distinct contributors, distinct downloaders, distinct site views, net change in membership, and Web site reporting.

XML-based Web services   A seamless way for objects on a server to accept incoming request from clients using the Internet's lowest common denominator of Hypertext Transfer Protocol/Extensible Markup Language (HTTP/XML).

Index

Susan D. Conway

Susan D. Conway is currently Group Program Manager for Microsoft Consulting Services, Knowledge Management. She completed her bachelor's and master's level work at California State University and has a Ph.D. in education from Columbia Pacific University. Her current work includes measurement and valuation of online communities and knowledge management. She has spent a number of years developing and managing corporate skills, resource allocation, and technical project management programs in large enterprises such as Texaco, Computer Sciences Corporation, NCR, and Microsoft. Her skills management work was quoted in *CIO* magazine—January 15, 1997, "The Skills that Thrill"—and her article on "Valuing Knowledge Management Behaviors" was presented at the World Congress on Intellectual Capital in January of 2002.

Char Sligar

Char Sligar is currently Program Manager for Microsoft Consulting Services— Knowledge Management. Her responsibilities include leading, managing, and mentoring knowledge management communities for Microsoft's consulting division. Char has an extensive background as a knowledge and education manager for both growth-stage software companies and Fortune 500 corporations. She holds a bachelor's degree from the University of Washington.

The manuscript for this book was prepared and galleyed using Microsoft Word Version 2002. Pages were composed by Microsoft Press using Adobe FrameMaker+SGML for Windows, with text and display type in ITC Clearface. Composed pages were delivered to the printer as electronic pre-press files.

Cover Designer:	Hornall Anderson Design Works	Project Manager:	Erin Connaughton
		Copy Editor:	Joseph Gustaitis
Interior Graphic Designer:	Joel Panchot	Technical Editor:	Robert Hogan
Principal Compositor:	Joanna Zito	Principal Proofreader:	Renée Cote
Interior Graphic Artist:	Beth McDermott	Indexer:	Edwin Durbin

Get a **Free**
e-mail newsletter, updates,
special offers, links to related books,
and more when you

register on line!

Register your Microsoft Press® title on our Web site and you'll get a FREE subscription to our e-mail newsletter, *Microsoft Press Book Connections.* You'll find out about newly released and upcoming books and learning tools, online events, software downloads, special offers and coupons for Microsoft Press customers, and information about major Microsoft® product releases. You can also read useful additional information about all the titles we publish, such as detailed book descriptions, tables of contents and indexes, sample chapters, links to related books and book series, author biographies, and reviews by other customers.

Registration is easy. Just visit this Web page and fill in your information:

http://www.microsoft.com/mspress/register

Microsoft

- -